CUSTOMS ACT (CANADA) 2018 EDITION

Updated as of February 26, 2018

THE LAW LIBRARY

TABLE OF CONTENTS

An Act respecting Customs	9
Customs Act	9
Short Title	9
Interpretation	9
PART I	13
General	13
Application to Her Majesty	13
Penalty and Interest	14
Security	14
Payment of Large Amounts	15
Performance of Obligations	15
Customs Offices and Facilities	15
Application of Act	16
Provision of Information	16
Forms	17
Electronic Filing	17
Brokers and Agents	18
PART II	19
Importation	19
Persons	19
Report of Goods	22
Duties	25
Liability for Duties on Goods Reported	25
Movement and Storage of Goods	25
Transportation	27
Warehouses and Duty Free Shops	28
Release	30
Accounting and Payment of Duties	30
Marking of Goods	34
Origin of Goods	35
Abandoned Goods	36
Unclaimed Goods	36

Goods of a Prescribed Class	37
Records	37
Verifications	39
Verifications under a Free Trade Agreement	39
Conduct of Verification	39
Statement of Origin	40
Effective Date of Re-determination of Origin	40
Denial or Withdrawal of Benefit of Preferential Tariff Treatment Under Certain Free Trade Agreements	41
Production of Documents	42
Advance Rulings	42
PART III	43
Calculation of Duty	43
Duties Based on Percentage Rates	43
Valuation for Duty	43
Interpretation	43
Determination of Value for Duty	44
Order of Consideration of Methods of Valuation	44
Transaction Value of the Goods	45
Transaction Value of Identical Goods	47
Transaction Value of Similar Goods	48
Deductive Value	48
Computed Value	50
Residual Method	50
General	51
Duties Based on Specific Quantities or Specific Values	51
Marking Determination	51
Determination, Re-determination and Further Re-determination of Origin, Tariff Classification and Value for Duty of Imported Goods	51
Re-determination and Further Re-determination by President	53
Appeals and References	56
Special Provisions	58
PART IV	59
Abatements and Refunds	59
PART V	63

Exportation	63
PART V.1	65
Collections	65
Interpretation	65
Ancillary Powers	66
General	66
Certificates, Liens and Set-off	67
Garnishment and Non-arm's Length Transfers	70
Acquisition of Property and Seizures	73
Collection Restrictions	74
Trustees, Receivers and Personal Representatives	75
Amalgamations and Windings-up	78
Partnerships	79
Unincorporated Bodies	79
Assessments, Objections and Appeals	79
Assessments	79
Objections and Appeals	81
PART VI	84
Enforcement	84
Powers of Officers	84
Limitation of Actions or Proceedings	88
Disclosure of Information	89
Inquiries	93
Penalties and Interest	94
Seizures	95
Return of Goods Seized	97
Forfeitures	99
General	99
Ascertained Forfeiture	99
Review of Seizure, Ascertained Forfeiture or Penalty Assessment	101
Third Party Claims	105
Disposal of Things Abandoned or Forfeit	108
Collection of Duties on Mail	109
Evidence	110

Prohibitions, Offences and Punishment	112
General	112
Procedure	114
PART VI.1	114
Enforcement of Criminal Offences Other than Offences Under This Act	114
Powers of Designated Officers	114
PART VII	115
Regulations	115
Parliamentary Review	117
Transitional	117
Consequential Amendments	117
Coming into Force	118
PART 1	118
PART 2	118
PART 3	118
PART 4	118
PART 5	118
RELATED PROVISIONS	118
— 1990, c. 16, s. 24(1)	118
— 1990, c. 17, s. 45(1)	118
— 1992, c. 28, ss. 2(2), (3)	118
— 1992, c. 28, ss. 2(2), (3)	119
— 1992, c. 28, s. 3(2)	119
— 1992, c. 28, s. 4(2)	119
— 1992, c. 28, s. 5(2)	119
— 1992, c. 28, s. 7(2)	119
— 1992, c. 28, s. 7(4)	119
— 1992, c. 28, s. 8(3)	120
— 1992, c. 28, s. 9(2)	120
— 1992, c. 28, s. 10(2)	120
— 1992, c. 28, s. 11(2)	120
— 1992, c. 28, s. 12(2)	120
— 1992, c. 28, s. 13(2)	120
— 1992, c. 28, s. 14(3)	120

— 1992, c. 28, s. 15(2)	120
— 1992, c. 28, s. 16(3)	120
— 1992, c. 28, s. 17(2)	120
— 1992, c. 28, s. 18(2)	121
— 1992, c. 28, s. 19(2)	121
— 1992, c. 28, s. 20(2)	121
— 1992, c. 28, s. 21(2)	121
— 1992, c. 28, s. 22(4)	121
— 1992, c. 28, s. 23(2)	121
— 1992, c. 28, ss. 24(2), (3)	121
— 1992, c. 28, ss. 24(2), (3)	121
— 1992, c. 28, s. 26(2)	121
— 1992, c. 28, s. 27(2)	122
— 1992, c. 28, s. 29(2)	122
— 1992, c. 28, s. 30(5)	122
— 1992, c. 28, s. 31(2)	122
— 1993, c. 25, ss. 90, 91(1)	122
— 1993, c. 25, ss. 90, 91(1)	122
— 1997, c. 26, s. 74(6)	122
— 1997, c. 26, s. 75(3)	122
— 1997, c. 26, s. 76(3)	122
— 1997, c. 26, s. 87(3)	123
— 1998, c. 19, s. 262(2)	123
— 1998, c. 30, s. 10	123
— 2000, c. 30, s. 161(2)	123
— 2001, c. 16, s. 44	123
— 2001, c. 25, s. 58(2)	123
— 2002, c. 22, ss. 305 to 308	123
— 2002, c. 22, ss. 305 to 308	123
— 2002, c. 22, ss. 305 to 308	124
— 2002, c. 22, ss. 305 to 308	124
— 2002, c. 22, s. 317	125
— 2003, c. 15, s. 59	125
— 2006, c. 4, s. 42	125

— 2006, c. 4, s. 50 — 125
— 2007, c. 35, s. 209 — 126
— 2008, c. 28, s. 49(3) — 126
— 2008, c. 28, s. 69 — 126
— 2008, c. 28, s. 70(2) — 126
— 2010, c. 12, s. 54 — 126
— 2017, c. 20, s. 67 — 126
AMENDMENTS NOT IN FORCE — 127
— 2009, c. 10, s. 5 — 127
— 2012, c. 24, s. 92 — 127
— 2014, c. 20, s. 366(1) — 127
— 2015, c. 27, s. 35 — 127
— 2017, c. 11, s. 7 — 128
— 2017, c. 27, s. 63 — 128

An Act respecting Customs

Customs Act

Short Title

Short title
1 This Act may be cited as the Customs Act

Interpretation

Definitions
2 (1) In this Act,
Agency
bonded warehouse
Customs Tariff
Canada
Canada-United States Free Trade Agreement
carrier code
CCFTA
Canada-Chile Free Trade Agreement Implementation Act
CCOFTA
Canada–Colombia Free Trade Agreement Implementation Act
CCRFTA
Canada — Costa Rica Free Trade Agreement Implementation Act
CEFTA
Canada–EFTA Free Trade Agreement Implementation Act
Certificate of Origin
CETA
Canada–European Union Comprehensive Economic and Trade Agreement Implementation Act
CHFTA
Canada–Honduras Economic Growth and Prosperity Act
Chile
Customs Tariff
CIFTA
Canada-Israel Free Trade Agreement Implementation Act
cigar
CJFTA
Canada–Jordan Economic Growth and Prosperity Act
CKFTA
Canada–Korea Economic Growth and Prosperity Act
Colombia
Customs Tariff
Commissioner
conveyance
Costa Rica
Customs Tariff
courier
CPAFTA

Canada–Panama Economic Growth and Prosperity Act
CPFTA
Canada–Peru Free Trade Agreement Implementation Act
CUFTA
Canada–Ukraine Free Trade Agreement Implementation Act
customs office
data
Deputy Minister
designated goods
(a) (b) aviation fuel,
(c) aviation gasoline,
(d) beer or malt liquor,
(e) diamonds,
(f) diesel fuel,
(g) gasoline,
(h) pearls,
(i) precious and semi-precious stones,
(i.1) spirits,
(j) wine, or
(k) such other goods as the Minister may, by order, designate for the purposes of all or any of the provisions of this Act; (
duties
Customs Tariff
Excise Act, 2001
Excise Tax Act
Special Import Measures Act
Excise Tax Act
duty free shop
EFTA state
Canada–EFTA Free Trade Agreement Implementation Act
EU country or other CETA beneficiary
Customs Tariff
excise stamp
Excise Act, 2001
export
forfeit
free trade agreement
free trade partner
goods
Honduras
Customs Tariff
Iceland
Customs Tariff
import
imported from Israel or another CIFTA beneficiary
Customs Tariff
inland waters
(a) from Cap-des-Rosiers to the westernmost point of Anticosti Island, and
(b) from Anticosti Island to the north shore of the St. Lawrence River along the meridian of longitude sixty-three degrees west; (
internal waters
Israel or another CIFTA beneficiary

Customs Tariff
Jordan
Customs Tariff
Korea
Customs Tariff
licensed user
Excise Act, 2001
Liechtenstein
Customs Tariff
mail
Canada Post Corporation Act
manufactured tobacco
Minister
NAFTA
North American Free Trade Agreement Implementation Act
NAFTA country
North American Free Trade Agreement Implementation Act
Norway
Customs Tariff
officer
Customs Tariff
Special Import Measures Act
Panama
Customs Tariff
person
Peru
Customs Tariff
preferential tariff treatment
preferential tariff treatment under CCFTA
preferential tariff treatment under CCOFTA
preferential tariff treatment under CCRFTA
preferential tariff treatment under CEFTA
preferential tariff treatment under CIFTA
preferential tariff treatment under CPFTA
preferential tariff treatment under NAFTA
prescribed
(a) in respect of a form or the manner of filing a form, authorized by the Minister,
(b) in respect of the information to be provided on or with a form, specified by the Minister, and
(c) in any other case, prescribed by regulation or determined in accordance with rules prescribed by regulation; (
President
Canada Border Services Agency Act
raw leaf tobacco
Excise Act, 2001
record
regulation
release
(a) in respect of goods, to authorize the removal of the goods from a customs office, sufferance warehouse, bonded warehouse or duty free shop for use in Canada, and
(b) in respect of goods to which paragraph 32(2)(b) applies, to receive the goods at the place of business of the importer, owner or consignee; (
restricted formulation

Excise Act, 2001
specially denatured alcohol
Excise Act, 2001
specified rate
spirits
Excise Act, 2001
spirits licensee
Excise Act, 2001
sufferance warehouse
Switzerland
Customs Tariff
tariff classification
Customs Tariff
territorial sea
tobacco licensee
Excise Act, 2001
tobacco product
Excise Act, 2001
Ukraine
Customs Tariff
United States
value for duty
wine
Excise Act, 2001
wine licensee
Excise Act, 2001

Definitions
(1.1) For the purpose of the definition
alcohol
ethyl alcohol
spirits
beer
malt liquor
Excise Act
diamonds
Customs Tariff
diesel fuel
Excise Tax Act
gasoline
Excise Tax Act
pearls
Customs Tariff
precious and semi-precious stones
Customs Tariff
wine

(1.2) Electronic records
(1.3) Every person required by this Act to keep records who does so electronically shall retain them in an electronically readable format for the prescribed retention period.

Restriction of Canadian waters
(2) The Governor in Council may from time to time by regulation temporarily restrict, for the purposes of this Act, the extent of Canadian waters, including the inland waters, but no such regulation shall be construed as foregoing any Canadian rights in respect of waters so restricted.

Powers, duties and functions of President
(3) Any power, duty or function of the President under this Act may be exercised or performed by any person, or by any officer within a class of officers, authorized by the President to do so and, if so exercised or performed, is deemed to have been exercised or performed by the President.
Delegation
(4) The Minister may authorize an officer or a class of officers to exercise powers or perform duties of the Minister, including any judicial or quasi-judicial powers or duties of the Minister, under this Act.
Delegation by Minister
(5) The Minister may authorize a person employed by the Canada Revenue Agency, or a class of those persons, to exercise powers or perform duties of the Minister, including any judicial or quasi-judicial powers or duties of the Minister, under this Act.
Delegation by Minister of National Revenue
(6) The Minister of National Revenue may authorize a person employed by the Canada Revenue Agency or the Agency, or a class of those persons, to exercise powers or perform duties of that Minister, including any judicial or quasi-judicial powers or duties of that Minister, under this Act.
R.S., 1985, c. 1 (2nd Supp.), s. 2, c. 41 (3rd Supp.), s. 118;
1988, c. 65, s. 66;
1990, c. 45, s. 19;
1992, c. 28, s. 1;
1993, c. 25, s. 68, c. 27, s. 213, c. 44, s. 81;
1994, c. 13, s. 7;
1995, c. 15, s. 24, c. 41, s. 1;
1996, c. 31, s. 73, c. 33, s. 28;
1997, c. 14, s. 35, c. 36, s. 147;
1998, c. 19, s. 262;
1999, c. 17, s. 123;
2001, c. 25, s. 1, c. 28, s. 26;
2002, c. 22, s. 328;
2005, c. 38, ss. 60, 145;
2007, c. 18, s. 135;
2009, c. 6, s. 23, c. 10, s. 1(F), c. 16, ss. 31, 56;
2010, c. 4, s. 25, c. 12, s. 48;
2012, c. 18, s. 24, c. 26, ss. 30, 62, c. 31, s. 264;
2014, c. 14, s. 23, c. 28, s. 26;
2017, c. 6, s. 82, c. 8, s. 20.

PART I

PART I
General

Application to Her Majesty

Duties binding on Her Majesty
3 (1) All duties or taxes levied on imported goods under the
Customs Tariff
Excise Act, 2001
Excise Tax Act
Special Import Measures Act
Act binding on Her Majesty
(2) Subject to subsection (3), this Act is binding on Her Majesty in right of Canada or a province.

Exemption
(3) The Governor in Council may by regulation exempt Her Majesty in any case or class of cases from the requirement to report under section 12 or 95 subject to such conditions as may be prescribed.
R.S., 1985, c. 1 (2nd Supp.), s. 3;
2002, c. 22, s. 329.

Penalty and Interest

Interest to be compounded
3.1 Interest shall be computed at a prescribed rate or at a specified rate and compounded daily and, if interest is computed in respect of an amount under a provision of this Act and is unpaid on the day it would, but for this section, have ceased to be computed under that provision, interest at the specified rate shall be computed and compounded daily on that unpaid interest from that day to the day it is paid and shall be paid as that provision required the amount to be paid.
1992, c. 28, s. 2;
2001, c. 25, s. 2.

Prescribed rate may be authorized
3.2 Where a person is required under a provision of this Act to pay interest on an amount at the specified rate, the person shall, where the Minister or any officer designated by the Minister for the purposes of this section so authorizes, pay interest on that amount under that provision at the prescribed rate rather than at the specified rate.
1992, c. 28, s. 2.

Waiver of penalty or interest
3.3 (1) Except with respect to the collection of any debt due to Her Majesty under Part V.1, the Minister or any officer designated by the President for the purposes of this section may at any time waive or cancel all or any portion of any penalty or interest otherwise payable by a person under this Act.

Exception
(1.1) Subsection (1) does not apply if measures may be taken under section 127.1, a request under section 129 is made or the time for making a request set out in that section has not expired.

Interest on penalty or interest refunded
(2) Where, as a result of a waiver or cancellation under subsection (1), a person is given a refund of an amount of penalty or interest that was paid by the person, the person shall be given, in addition to the refund, interest at the prescribed rate for the period beginning on the first day after the day the amount was paid and ending on the day the refund is given, calculated on the amount of the refund.
1992, c. 28, s. 2;
1995, c. 41, s. 2;
2001, c. 25, s. 3;
2005, c. 38, s. 61.

Security

Additional security
3.4 (1) Where security has been given to the Minister by a person under a provision of this Act and the Minister or any officer (in this section referred to as a "designated officer") designated by the President for the purposes of this section determines that the security that has been given is no longer adequate, the Minister or a designated officer may, by notice served personally or by registered or certified mail, require additional security to be given by or on behalf of the person within such reasonable time as may be stipulated in the notice.

Payment where additional security not given
(2) Where the additional security required to be given by or on behalf of a person under subsection

(1) is not given within the time it is so required to be given, the amount by which
(a) the amount owing in respect of which security that has been given to the Minister by the person is no longer adequate
exceeds
(b) the value of the security that has been given to the Minister by the person, as determined by the Minister or a designated officer,
is payable by the person immediately.
1992, c. 28, s. 2;
2005, c. 38, s. 62.

Payment of Large Amounts

Where excess amount to be paid
3.5 Except in the circumstances that the Minister may specify, every person who makes a payment of any amount under this Act shall, if the amount exceeds the amount specified by the Minister, make the payment to the account of the Receiver General in the prescribed manner and within the prescribed time at
(a) a bank;
(b) a credit union;
(c) a corporation authorized by an Act of Parliament or of the legislature of a province to carry on the business of offering its services as a trustee to the public; or
(d) a corporation authorized by an Act of Parliament or of the legislature of a province to accept deposits from the public and that carries on the business of lending money on the security of real property or immovables or of investing in mortgages or hypothecary claims on immovables.
2001, c. 25, s. 4.

Performance of Obligations

Performance of obligations
4 Where more than one person is responsible for the performance of any obligation under this Act, performance of the obligation by any one of them shall be deemed to be performance by all of them.
Undertakings
4.1 In the case of goods to which paragraph 32(2)(b) applies, the Minister may accept from an importer or transporter an undertaking to assume obligations in relation to compliance with this Act and the regulations.
2001, c. 25, s. 5.

Customs Offices and Facilities

Customs offices
5 The Minister may designate customs offices inside or outside Canada for a specified purpose or generally for business relating to customs and may at any time amend, cancel or reinstate any such designation.
Customs facilities
6 (1) The owner or operator of
(a) any international bridge or tunnel, for the use of which a toll or other charge is payable,
(b) any railway operating internationally, or
(c) any airport, wharf or dock that receives conveyances operating internationally and in respect of which a customs office has been designated under section 5
shall provide, equip and maintain free of charge to Her Majesty at or near the bridge, tunnel, railway, airport, wharf or dock adequate buildings, accommodation or other facilities for the proper detention and examination of imported goods or for the proper search of persons by customs officers.

Clarification
(1.1) For the purposes of subsection (1), maintain
Retroactive effect
(1.2) Subsection (1.1) has retroactive effect to the day on which subsection (1) came into force and applies in respect of any action or judicial proceeding that is pending on the day on which this subsection comes into force.
Rights of Minister
(2) The Minister may
(a) make such improvements as the Minister considers desirable to any facilities provided pursuant to subsection (1),
(b) post, on or about such facilities, such signs as the Minister considers appropriate for the safe use of the facilities or for the enforcement of any law relating to the importation or exportation of goods or the international movement of persons, and
(c) continue to use such facilities for as long a period of time as the Minister requires,
and no person shall interfere with any of the rights set out in this subsection.
Regulations
(3) The Governor in Council may, subject to subsection (4), make regulations determining what are adequate buildings, accommodation and other facilities for the purposes referred to in subsection (1).
Retroactive effect of regulations
(3.1) A regulation made under subsection (3) may, if it so provides, have retroactive effect and apply in respect of any pending action or judicial proceeding.
Canada Labour Code
(4) Any building, accommodation or other facility provided for the purposes referred to in subsection (1) that fails to meet the applicable requirements of Part II of the
Canada Labour Code
Powers of Minister
(5) Where any building, accommodation or other facility provided pursuant to subsection (1) at or near an international bridge or tunnel is not adequate for the purposes referred to in that subsection, the Minister may, on thirty days notice to the owner or operator of the bridge or tunnel, carry out any construction or repairs on the site of the facility in order to render it adequate for those purposes.
Liability for costs
(6) The owner or operator of an international bridge or tunnel is liable for all reasonable costs incurred by the Minister under subsection (5), which costs may be recovered in accordance with sections 143 to 145.
R.S., 1985, c. 1 (2nd Supp.), s. 6, c. 26 (3rd Supp.), s. 1;
2012, c. 31, s. 265.

Application of Act

Application inside and outside Canada
7 Subject to this Act and the regulations, any of the powers, duties or functions established under this Act or the regulations relating to the importation of goods may be carried out inside Canada or, where they do not conflict with the laws of another country, inside that other country and may be carried out before or after the importation.

Provision of Information

Obligation to provide accurate information
7.1 Any information provided to an officer in the administration or enforcement of this Act, the Customs Tariff
Special Import Measures Act

2001, c. 25, s. 6.

Forms

Declaration
8 The Minister may include on any form a declaration, to be signed by the person completing the form, declaring that the information given by that person on the form is true, accurate and complete.
R.S., 1985, c. 1 (2nd Supp.), s. 8;
2001, c. 25, s. 7.

Electronic Filing

Meaning of
electronic filing
8.1 (1) For the purposes of this section,
electronic filing
Application for electronic filing
(2) A person who is required to file or otherwise provide forms under this Act or the
Customs Tariff
Authorization
(3) If the Minister is satisfied that a person who files an application under subsection (2) meets the criteria referred to in that subsection, the Minister may, in writing, authorize the person to file or otherwise provide forms by way of electronic filing, subject to such conditions as the Minister may at any time impose.
Revocation
(4) The Minister may revoke an authorization granted to a person under subsection (3) if
(a) the person, in writing, requests the Minister to revoke the authorization;
(b) the person fails to comply with any condition imposed in respect of the authorization or any provision of this Act or the
Customs Tariff
(c) the Minister is no longer satisfied that the criteria referred to in subsection (2) are met; or
(d) the Minister considers that the authorization is no longer required.
Notice of revocation
(5) If the Minister revokes the authorization, the Minister shall notify the person in writing of the revocation and its effective date.
Deemed filing
(6) For the purposes of this Act and the
Customs Tariff
Print-outs as evidence
(7) For the purposes of this Act and the
Customs Tariff
Regulations
(8) The Governor in Council may, on the recommendation of the Minister, make regulations in respect of electronic systems or any other technology to be used in the administration of this Act or the
Customs Tariff
(a) the supplying of information or forms for any purpose under this Act or the
Customs Tariff
(b) the payment of amounts under this Act or the
Customs Tariff
(c) the manner in which and the extent to which, if at all, any provision of this Act or the
Customs Tariff

1997, c. 36, s. 148;
2001, c. 25, s. 8.

Brokers and Agents

Issue of customs broker's licence
9 (1) Subject to the regulations, the Minister or any person designated by the Minister for the purposes of this section may issue to any person who is qualified under the regulations a licence to transact business as a customs broker.

Amendment, etc., of licence
(2) Subject to the regulations, the Minister may amend, suspend, renew, cancel or reinstate any licence issued under subsection (1), and any person designated by the Minister for the purpose of this section may amend, suspend, renew, cancel or reinstate any licence issued by himself under subsection (1).

Records
(3) If an officer so requests, a customs broker shall make available to the officer, within the time specified by the officer, any records that the customs broker is required by the regulations to keep.

Prohibition
(4) No person shall transact or attempt to transact business as a customs broker or hold himself out as a customs broker unless the person holds a licence issued under subsection (1) or unless he is qualified under the regulations and is duly authorized to transact business as a customs broker by a person who holds such a licence, but nothing in this subsection shall be so construed as to prohibit any person from transacting business on his own behalf under this Act, or to prohibit persons administering estates or other duly authorized agents from transacting business under this Act.

Regulations
(5) The Governor in Council may make regulations
(a) prescribing qualifications as to citizenship, residence and knowledge of the laws and procedures relating to importations and exportations and any other qualifications that must be met by an applicant for a customs broker's licence issued under subsection (1), and any such qualifications that must be met by a person who transacts business as a customs broker on behalf of a person so licensed;
(b) prescribing the terms and conditions on which such licences may be issued, including the security that may be required and the fees, if any, to be paid for the licences;
(c) prescribing the duration of such licences;
(d) prescribing the manner of applying for such licences or for renewals thereof;
(e) providing for the examination of applicants for such licences, and of persons who will transact business as customs brokers on their behalf, by the Minister or by any other person with respect to their knowledge of the laws and procedures relating to importations and exportations;
(f) prescribing the examination fees to be paid, the amount of any deposit that may be taken in respect thereof and the conditions under which such fees or deposits may be refunded;
(g) prescribing the records to be kept by customs brokers and the period of time for which they shall be kept; and
(h) prescribing the manner and circumstances in which the Minister may suspend or cancel a customs broker's licence issued under subsection (1) or any other person may suspend or cancel such a licence issued by himself thereunder, and the circumstances in which a customs broker's licence shall be surrendered.
R.S., 1985, c. 1, (2nd Supp.), s. 9;
2001, c. 25, s. 9.

Agents
10 (1) Subject to the regulations, any person who is duly authorized to do so may transact business under this Act as the agent of another person, but an officer may refuse to transact business with any such person unless that person, on the request of the officer, produces a written authority, in a form

approved by the Minister, from the person on whose behalf he is acting.
Administrators
(2) Any person who is duly authorized to administer the estate of another person by reason of death, bankruptcy, insolvency or incapacity or for any other reason may transact business under this Act on behalf of the estate but an officer may refuse to transact business with any such person unless that person satisfies the officer that he is duly authorized to administer the estate.
Regulations
(3) The Governor in Council may make regulations in respect of any provision of this Act prescribing the circumstances in which a person may transact business under that provision as the agent of another person.

PART II

PART II
Importation

Persons

Presentation of persons on arrival in Canada
11 (1) Subject to this section, every person arriving in Canada shall, except in such circumstances and subject to such conditions as may be prescribed, enter Canada only at a customs office designated for that purpose that is open for business and without delay present himself or herself to an officer and answer truthfully any questions asked by the officer in the performance of his or her duties under this or any other Act of Parliament.
Exception
(2) Subsection (1) does not apply to any person who has presented himself or herself outside Canada at a customs office designated for that purpose and has not subsequently stopped at any other place prior to his or her arrival in Canada unless an officer requires that person to present himself or herself to the officer.
Presentation of passengers and crew
(3) Subject to this section, every person in charge of a conveyance arriving in Canada shall, except in such circumstances and subject to such conditions as may be prescribed, ensure that the passengers and crew are forthwith on arrival in Canada transported to a customs office referred to in subsection (1).
Exception
(4) Subsection (3) does not apply to any person in charge of a conveyance transporting passengers and crew all of whom have presented themselves outside Canada at a customs office designated for that purpose and have not subsequently stopped at any other place prior to their arrival in Canada unless an officer requires that person to comply therewith.
Entry and departure
(5) Subject to the regulations, subsections (1) and (3) do not apply to any of the following persons, unless an officer requires them to comply with those subsections:
(a) a person who enters Canadian waters, including the inland waters, or the airspace over Canada on board a conveyance directly from outside Canada and then leaves Canada on board the conveyance, as long as the person was continuously on board that conveyance while in Canada and
(i) in the case of a conveyance other than an aircraft, the person did not land in Canada and the conveyance did not anchor, moor or make contact with another conveyance while in Canadian waters, including the inland waters, or
(ii) in the case of an aircraft, the conveyance did not land while in Canada; and
(b) a person who leaves Canadian waters, including the inland waters, or the airspace over Canada on board a conveyance and then re-enters Canada on board the conveyance, as long as the person was continuously on board that conveyance while outside Canada and

(i) in the case of a conveyance other than an aircraft, the person did not land outside Canada and the conveyance did not anchor, moor or make contact with another conveyance while outside Canada, or
(ii) in the case of an aircraft, the conveyance did not land while outside Canada.

Exception — alternative manner

(6) Subsection (1) does not apply to a person who
(a) holds an authorization issued by the Minister under subsection 11.1(1) to present himself or herself in a prescribed alternative manner and who presents himself or herself in the manner authorized for that person; or
(b) is a member of a prescribed class of persons authorized by regulations made under subsection 11.1(3) to present himself or herself in a prescribed alternative manner and who presents himself or herself in the manner authorized for that class.

Powers of officer

(7) Notwithstanding that a person holds an authorization under subsection 11.1(1) or is authorized under the regulations made under subsection 11.1(3), an officer may require a person to present himself or herself in accordance with subsection (1).

R.S., 1985, c. 1 (2nd Supp.), s. 11;
1996, c. 31, s. 74;
2001, c. 25, s. 10;
2012, c. 19, s. 372;
2017, c. 11, s. 2.

Minister may authorize

11.1 (1) Subject to the regulations, the Minister may issue to any person an authorization to present himself or herself in an alternative manner.

Amendment, etc., of authorization

(2) The Minister may, subject to the regulations, amend, suspend, renew, cancel or reinstate an authorization.

Regulations

(3) The Governor in Council may make regulations
(a) prescribing classes of persons who are, and classes of persons who may be, authorized to present themselves in alternative manners;
(b) respecting alternative manners of presentation;
(c) respecting the requirements and conditions that are to be met before authorizations may be issued;
(d) respecting the terms and conditions of authorizations;
(e) respecting the amendment, suspension, renewal, cancellation or reinstatement of authorizations; and
(f) respecting fees or the manner of determining fees to be paid for authorizations.

Service Fees Act

(4) The
Service Fees Act
2001, c. 25, s. 11;
2010, c. 25, s. 172;
2012, c. 19, s. 373;
2017, c. 20, s. 454.

Designation of customs controlled areas

11.2 (1) The Minister may designate an area as a customs controlled area for the purposes of this section and sections 11.3 to 11.5 and 99.2 and 99.3.

Amendment, etc. of designation

(2) The Minister may amend, cancel or reinstate at any time a designation made under this section.
2001, c. 25, s. 11.

Entry prohibited

11.3 (1) No owner or operator of a facility where a customs controlled area is located shall grant or

allow to be granted access to the customs controlled area to any person unless the person
(a) has been authorized by the Minister; or
(b) is a prescribed person or a member of a prescribed class of persons.
Amendment, etc., of authorization
(2) The Minister may amend, suspend, renew, cancel or reinstate an authorization.
2001, c. 25, s. 11;
2009, c. 10, s. 2.
Presentation and reporting — when leaving customs controlled area
11.4 (1) Subject to subsection (2), every person who is leaving a customs controlled area shall, if requested to do so by an officer,
(a) present himself or herself in the prescribed manner to an officer and identify himself or herself;
(b) report in the prescribed manner any goods that he or she has acquired through any means while in the customs controlled area;
(b.1) present those goods and remove any covering from them, unload any conveyance or open any part of it, or open or unpack any package or container that an officer wishes to examine; and
(c) answer truthfully any questions asked by an officer in the performance of his or her duties under this or any other Act of Parliament.
Presentation and reporting — within customs controlled area
(1.1) Every person who is in a customs controlled area shall, if requested to do so by an officer,
(a) present himself or herself in the prescribed manner to an officer and identify himself or herself; and
(b) answer truthfully any questions asked by an officer in the performance of his or her duties under this or any other Act of Parliament.
Non-application of subsections (1) and (1.1)
(2) Subsections (1) and (1.1) do not apply to persons who are required to present themselves under section 11 or report goods under section 12.
2001, c. 25, s. 11;
2009, c. 10, s. 3.
Regulations
11.5 The Governor in Council may make regulations
(a) prescribing the persons or classes of persons who may be granted access under paragraph 11.3(1)(b); and
(b) respecting the manner in which a person must present himself or herself under paragraphs 11.4(1)(a) and (1.1)(a) and report goods under paragraph 11.4(1)(b).
(c) to (e) 2001, c. 25, s. 11;
2009, c. 10, s. 4.
Designation of mixed-traffic corridor
11.6 (1) If the Minister considers that it is necessary in the public interest, he or she may designate as a mixed-traffic corridor a portion of a roadway or other access way that
(a) leads from an international border to a customs office designated under section 5; and
(b) is used by persons arriving in Canada and by persons travelling within Canada.
Amendment, etc., of designation
(2) The Minister may amend, cancel or reinstate at any time a designation made under this section.
2012, c. 19, s. 481.
Person travelling in mixed-traffic corridor
11.7 Every person who is travelling in a mixed-traffic corridor shall present themselves to an officer at the nearest customs office and state whether they are arriving from a location outside or within Canada.
2012, c. 19, s. 481.

Report of Goods

Report
12 (1) Subject to this section, all goods that are imported shall, except in such circumstances and subject to such conditions as may be prescribed, be reported at the nearest customs office designated for that purpose that is open for business.
Time and manner of report
(2) Goods shall be reported under subsection (1) at such time and in such manner as the Governor in Council may prescribe.
Who reports
(3) Goods shall be reported under subsection (1)
(a) in the case of goods in the actual possession of a person arriving in Canada, or that form part of the person's baggage where the person and the person's baggage are being carried on board the same conveyance, by that person or, in prescribed circumstances, by the person in charge of the conveyance;
(a.1) in the case of goods imported by courier or as mail, by the person who exported the goods to Canada;
(b) in the case of goods, other than goods referred to in paragraph (a) or goods imported as mail, on board a conveyance arriving in Canada, by the person in charge of the conveyance; and
(c) in any other case, by the person on behalf of whom the goods are imported.
Goods returned to Canada
(3.1) For greater certainty, for the purposes of the reporting of goods under subsection (1), the return of goods to Canada after they are taken out of Canada is an importation of those goods.
Where goods are reported outside Canada
(4) Subsection (1) does not apply in respect of goods that are reported in the manner prescribed under subsection (2) prior to importation at a customs office outside Canada unless an officer requires that the goods be reported again under subsection (1) after importation.
Exception — entry and departure
(5) Subject to the regulations, unless an officer otherwise requires, this section does not apply in respect of goods on board a conveyance
(a) that enters Canadian waters, including the inland waters, or the airspace over Canada directly from outside Canada and then leaves Canada, as long as
(i) in the case of a conveyance other than an aircraft, the conveyance did not anchor, moor or make contact with another conveyance while in Canadian waters, including the inland waters, or
(ii) in the case of an aircraft, the conveyance did not land while in Canada; or
(b) that leaves Canadian waters, including the inland waters, or the airspace over Canada and then re-enters Canada, as long as
(i) in the case of a conveyance other than an aircraft, the conveyance did not anchor, moor or make contact with another conveyance while outside Canada, or
(ii) in the case of an aircraft, the conveyance did not land while outside Canada.
Written report
(6) Where goods are required by the regulations to be reported under subsection (1) in writing, they shall be reported in the prescribed form containing the prescribed information, or in such form containing such information as is satisfactory to the Minister.
Certain goods not subject to seizure
(7) Goods described in tariff item No. 9813.00.00 or 9814.00.00 in the List of Tariff Provisions set out in the schedule to the
Customs Tariff
(a) that are in the actual possession of a person arriving in Canada, or that form part of his baggage, where the person and his baggage are being carried on board the same conveyance,
(b) that are not charged with duties, and
(c) the importation of which is not prohibited under the
Customs Tariff
may not be seized as forfeit under this Act by reason only that they were not reported under this

section.
R.S., 1985, c. 1 (2nd Supp.), s. 12, c. 41 (3rd Supp.), s. 119;
1992, c. 28, s. 3;
1996, c. 31, s. 75;
1997, c. 36, s. 149;
2001, c. 25, s. 12;
2015, c. 3, s. 60(F);
2017, c. 11, s. 3.
Regulations
12.01 The Governor in Council may make regulations for the purposes of sections 11 and 12, including regulations
(a) prescribing the circumstances under which persons, goods or classes thereof on board a conveyance, or classes thereof, are required to present themselves or to be reported, as the case may be, despite subsection 11(5) or 12(5); or
(b) defining the expression "make contact with another conveyance" for the purposes of subsections 11(5) and 12(5) and prescribing the circumstances under which a conveyance or a class thereof makes contact with another conveyance.
2017, c. 11, s. 4.
Advance information
12.1 (1) Before the arrival of a conveyance in Canada, the owner or person in charge of a conveyance who is prescribed or any other prescribed person shall give the Agency prescribed information about the conveyance and the persons and goods on board or expected to be on board the conveyance.
Exemption
(2) A person who is required to provide information under subsection (1) shall hold a valid carrier code unless they are exempt.
Carrier code — requirements
(3) An application for a carrier code shall be made in the prescribed form with the prescribed information.
Carrier code — issuance
(4) The Minister shall issue a carrier code to a person who applies for it if the application meets the requirements referred to in subsection (3) and the Minister is satisfied that the prescribed requirements and conditions for the carrier code to be issued have been met.
Carrier code — suspension, cancellation and reinstatement
(5) The Minister may, subject to the regulations, suspend, cancel or reinstate a carrier code.
Notification
(6) The Minister may issue a notification to any person who provides information under subsection (1) to require the person to take any specified measure with respect to the information.
Obligation to comply
(7) The person to whom a notification is issued shall comply with the notification.
Regulations
(8) The Governor in Council may make regulations for the purposes of this section, including regulations
(a) respecting the information that must be given under subsection (1);
(b) prescribing the persons or classes of persons who must give the information under subsection (1);
(c) respecting the circumstances in which the information must be given under subsection (1);
(d) respecting the time within which and the manner in which the information must be given under subsection (1);
(e) regarding the requirements and conditions that are to be met before a carrier code may be issued;
(f) regarding the persons or classes of persons who are exempt from holding a valid carrier code; and
(g) regarding the manner and circumstances in which a carrier code may be suspended, cancelled or reinstated.

2009, c. 10, s. 6;
2012, c. 31, s. 266.

Obligation to answer questions and present goods

13 Every person who reports goods under section 12 inside or outside Canada or is stopped by an officer in accordance with section 99.1 shall
(a) answer truthfully any question asked by an officer with respect to the goods; and
(b) if an officer so requests, present the goods to the officer, remove any covering from the goods, unload any conveyance or open any part of the conveyance, or open or unpack any package or container that the officer wishes to examine.
R.S., 1985, c. 1 (2nd Supp.), s. 13;
2001, c. 25, s. 13.

Restriction on unloading before report

14 (1) No person shall unload goods from a conveyance arriving in Canada until the goods have been reported in accordance with sections 12 and 13 except where the safety of the conveyance, or the goods or persons on the conveyance, is threatened by collision, fire, the stress of weather or other similar circumstances or in such other circumstances as may be prescribed.

Report of goods unloaded

(2) Where a conveyance is unloaded in the circumstances described in subsection (1), the person in charge of the conveyance shall forthwith, in such manner as may be prescribed, report the conveyance, the goods that were so unloaded and any goods that remain on the conveyance at a customs office designated for that purpose.

Report of goods illegally imported

15 Any person who finds or has in his possession goods that have been imported and who believes on reasonable grounds that the provisions of this or any other Act of Parliament that prohibits, controls or regulates the importation of goods have not been complied with in respect of the goods or that duties levied thereon have not been paid shall forthwith report to an officer that he has found the goods or has them in his possession.

Wreck deemed imported

16 (1) For the purposes of this Act, any wreck that has come into Canada from outside Canada shall be deemed to have been imported.

Report of wreck and liability for duties

(2) If any wreck that has come into Canada from outside Canada is released to a person under section 158 of the
Canada Shipping Act, 2001
(a) shall forthwith report the delivery to an officer; and
(b) is, from the time of the delivery, liable for all duties thereon calculated at the rates applicable to the wreck at the time of the delivery.

Definition of
wreck

(3) In this section,
wreck
(a) jetsam, flotsam, lagan and derelict found in, or on the shores of, the sea, any tidal water, or any of the inland waters;
(b) cargo, stores and tackle of any vessel and of all parts of the vessel separated therefrom;
(c) the property of shipwrecked persons; and
(d) any wrecked aircraft or any part thereof and cargo thereof.
R.S., 1985, c. 1 (2nd Supp.), s. 16;
2001, c. 26, s. 299.

Duties

Goods charged with duties from importation

17 (1) Imported goods are charged with duties thereon from the time of importation thereof until such time as the duties are paid or the charge is otherwise removed.
Rates of duties
(2) Subject to this Act, the rates of duties on imported goods shall be the rates applicable to the goods at the time they are accounted for under subsection 32(1), (2) or (5) or, where goods have been released in the circumstances set out in paragraph 32(2)(b), at the time of release.
Liability
(3) Whenever the importer of the goods that have been released or any person authorized under paragraph 32(6)(a) or subsection 32(7) to account for goods becomes liable under this Act to pay duties on those goods, the owner of the goods at the time of release becomes jointly and severally, or solidarily, liable, with the importer or person authorized, to pay the duties.
R.S., 1985, c. 1 (2nd Supp.), s. 17;
1992, c. 28, s. 4;
2001, c. 25, s. 14;
2004, c. 25, s. 120(E).

Liability for Duties on Goods Reported

Presumption of importation
18 (1) For the purposes of this section, all goods reported under section 12 shall be deemed to have been imported.
Liability of person reporting goods short landed
(2) Subject to subsections (3) and 20(2.1), any person who reports goods under section 12, and any person for whom that person acts as agent or employee while so reporting, are jointly and severally or solidarily liable for all duties levied on the goods unless one or the other of them proves, within the time that may be prescribed, that the duties have been paid or that the goods
(a) were destroyed or lost prior to report or destroyed after report but prior to receipt in a place referred to in paragraph (c) or by a person referred to in paragraph (d);
(b) did not leave the place outside Canada from which they were to have been exported;
(c) have been received in a customs office, sufferance warehouse, bonded warehouse or duty free shop;
(d) have been received by a person who transports or causes to be transported within Canada goods in accordance with subsection 20(1);
(e) have been exported; or
(f) have been released.
Rates of duties
(3) The rates of duties payable on goods under subsection (2) shall be the rates applicable to the goods at the time they were reported under section 12.
Regulations
(4) The Governor in Council may make regulations prescribing the circumstances in which such bonds or other security as may be prescribed may be required from any person who is or may become liable for the payment of duties under this section.
R.S., 1985, c. 1 (2nd Supp.), s. 18;
2001, c. 25, s. 15.

Movement and Storage of Goods

Disposition of goods before release
19 (1) Subject to section 20, any person who is authorized by an officer or by any prescribed means to do so may
(a) deliver goods that have been reported under section 12 or cause them to be delivered from a customs office to another customs office or a sufferance warehouse;

(b) deliver such goods or cause them to be delivered from a sufferance warehouse to another sufferance warehouse;
(c) where such goods are designated as ships' stores by regulations made under paragraph 99(g) of the
Customs Tariff
(d) export such goods or cause them to be exported directly from a customs office or sufferance warehouse; or
(e) where such goods are at a customs office, leave them at that office, subject to such storage charges as may be prescribed.

Authorization to deliver goods
(1.1) In prescribed circumstances and under prescribed conditions, a person may be authorized by an officer or by any prescribed means to deliver goods or cause them to be delivered to the place of business of the importer, owner or consignee.

Movement and storage of goods
(2) Subject to section 20, where goods that have been reported under section 12 have been described in the prescribed form at a customs office designated for that purpose, any person who is authorized by an officer or by any prescribed means to do so may
(a) deliver the goods or cause them to be delivered from a customs office or sufferance warehouse to a bonded warehouse or duty free shop;
(b) deliver them or cause them to be delivered from a bonded warehouse to another bonded warehouse or to a duty free shop or from a duty free shop to another duty free shop or to a bonded warehouse;
(c) where the goods are designated as ships' stores by regulations made under paragraph 99(g) of the Customs Tariff
(d) export them or cause them to be exported directly from a duty free shop in accordance with regulations made under section 30; or
(e) export them or cause them to be exported directly from a bonded warehouse.

Duties removed
(3) Goods that are removed as ships' stores under paragraph (1)(c) or exported under paragraph (1)(d) are, from the time of their exportation, no longer charged with duties.
(4) and (5) R.S., 1985, c. 1 (2nd Supp.), s. 19;
1993, c. 25, s. 69;
1995, c. 41, s. 3;
1997, c. 36, s. 150;
2001, c. 25, s. 16.

Statistics
19.1 (1) Subject to this section, any person who is authorized by an officer under subsection 19(2) to deliver goods or cause them to be delivered to a bonded warehouse shall, before the delivery, furnish an officer at a customs office with the statistical code for the goods determined by reference to the Coding System established pursuant to section 22.1 of the
Statistics Act

Prescribed form
(2) The statistical code referred to in subsection (1) shall be furnished in the prescribed manner and in the prescribed form containing the prescribed information.

Regulations
(3) The Governor in Council may make regulations exempting persons or goods, or classes thereof, from the requirements of subsection (1) subject to such conditions, if any, as are specified in the regulations.
1988, c. 65, s. 67.

Transportation

Transportation of goods
20 (1) Except in such circumstances as may be prescribed, every person who transports or causes to be transported within Canada goods that have been imported but have not been released shall do so subject to such conditions and subject to such bonds or other security as may be prescribed.

Liability of transporter
(2) Subject to subsection (2.1), every person who transports or causes to be transported within Canada goods, other than goods to which paragraph 32(2)(b) applies, that have been imported but have not been released is liable for all duties on the goods unless the person proves, within the time that may be prescribed, that the goods were
(a) destroyed while being so transported;
(b) received in a customs office, sufferance warehouse, bonded warehouse or duty free shop;
(c) where the goods are designated as ships' stores by regulations made under paragraph 99(g) of the Customs Tariff
(d) received by another person who is entitled under subsection (1) to transport such goods; or
(e) exported.

Exception
(2.1) If a person transports within Canada goods to which paragraph 32(2)(b) applies, which the person is required to report under section 12 but which have not been released, the person is liable for all duties on the goods unless the person proves, within the time that may be prescribed, that the goods were
(a) destroyed while being transported;
(b) received in a customs office, bonded warehouse or duty free shop;
(c) if the goods are designated as ships' stores by regulations made under paragraph 99(g) of the Customs Tariff
(d) exported; or
(e) received at the place of business of the importer, owner or consignee.

Rates of duties
(3) The rates of duties payable on goods under subsection (2) shall be the rates applicable to the goods at the time they were reported under section 12.
R.S., 1985, c. 1 (2nd Supp.), s. 20;
1995, c. 41, s. 4;
1997, c. 36, s. 151;
2001, c. 25, s. 17.

Officer's access to goods
21 Every person who transports or causes to be transported within Canada goods that have been imported but have not been released shall, where an officer so requests, afford the officer free access to any premises or place under his control that is attached to or forms part of any place where such goods are reported, loaded, unloaded or stored, and open any package or container of such goods or remove any covering therefrom.

Records
22 (1) Subject to subsection (2), the following persons shall keep the prescribed records at their place of business in Canada or at any other place that the Minister may designate, for the prescribed period and in the prescribed manner, and shall on the request of an officer make them available to the officer, within the time specified by the officer, and answer truthfully any questions asked by the officer about those records:
(a) a person who transports or causes to be transported goods into Canada; or
(b) a person who transports or causes to be transported within Canada goods that have been imported but have not been released.

Exemption
(2) The Minister may, subject to such terms and conditions as he may specify, exempt any person or class of persons from the requirement to keep records or from the requirement to keep records in Canada where he deems it unnecessary or impracticable to keep records or to keep them in Canada.

R.S., 1985, c. 1 (2nd Supp.), s. 22;
1995, c. 41, s. 5;
2001, c. 25, s. 18.

Transportation over territory outside Canada
23 Goods that are transported from one place in Canada to another place in Canada over territory or waters outside Canada in accordance with such terms and conditions and subject to such bonds or other security as may be prescribed shall be treated, with respect to their liability to or exemption from duties, as if they had been transported entirely within Canada.

Warehouses and Duty Free Shops

Licences
24 (1) Subject to the regulations, the Minister may, where he deems it necessary or desirable to do so, issue to any person qualified under the regulations a licence for the operation of any place
(a) as a sufferance warehouse for the examination of imported goods that have not been released, or
(b) (c) as a duty free shop for the sale of goods free of certain duties or taxes levied on goods under the
Customs Tariff
Excise Act
Excise Act, 2001
Excise Tax Act
Special Import Measures Act
and may specify in the licence any restriction as to the classes of goods that may be received therein or the circumstances in which goods may be received therein.

Definition of
duties
(1.1) The definition
duties

Amendment of licence
(2) The Minister may, subject to the regulations, amend, suspend, renew, cancel or reinstate a licence issued under subsection (1).
R.S., 1985, c. 1 (2nd Supp.), s. 24;
1993, c. 25, s. 70;
1995, c. 41, s. 6;
2001, c. 16, s. 2;
2002, c. 22, s. 330.

Sufferance warehouse operator's obligation
25 Subject to the regulations, the operator of a sufferance warehouse shall not refuse to receive any goods brought to the warehouse that qualify under the terms of his licence.

Price of goods sold in duty free shop
26 (1) The operator of a duty free shop shall ensure that the prices of goods offered for sale at the duty free shop reflect the extent to which the goods have not been subject to duties and taxes.

Definition
(2) In subsection (1),
duties
Customs Tariff
Excise Act
Excise Act, 2001
Excise Tax Act
Special Import Measures Act
R.S., 1985, c. 1 (2nd Supp.), s. 26;
1993, c. 25, s. 71;

2002, c. 22, s. 331.

Officer's access to goods

27 The operator of a sufferance warehouse, bonded warehouse or duty free shop shall, where an officer so requests, afford the officer free access to the warehouse or duty free shop or any premises or place under his control that is attached to or forms part of the warehouse or duty free shop and open any package or container of goods therein or remove any covering therefrom.

Liability of operator

28 (1) The operator of a sufferance warehouse, bonded warehouse or duty free shop is liable for all duties or taxes levied under the

Customs Tariff
Excise Act
Excise Act, 2001
Excise Tax Act
Special Import Measures Act

(a) are still in the warehouse or duty free shop;
(b) have been destroyed while in the warehouse or duty free shop;
(c) have been removed from the warehouse or duty free shop pursuant to section 19;
(d) have been taken as a sample or seized under the

Firearms Act

(e) have been released by an officer.

(1.1) and (1.2) Rates

(2) The rates of duties or taxes payable on goods under subsection (1) shall
(a) where the goods have been received in a sufferance warehouse, be the rates applicable to such goods at the time they were reported under section 12; and
(b) where the goods have been received in a bonded warehouse or duty free shop, be the rates applicable to such goods at the time they were received therein.

Definition of
duties
(3) The definition
duties

R.S., 1985, c. 1 (2nd Supp.), s. 28;
1993, c. 25, s. 72;
1995, c. 39, s. 168;
2001, c. 25, s. 19;
2002, c. 22, ss. 332, 408.

29 Regulations

30 The Governor in Council may make regulations
(a) prescribing qualifications as to citizenship and residence or any other qualifications that must be met by the operator of a sufferance warehouse or duty free shop;
(b) prescribing the terms and conditions on which licences for the operation of sufferance warehouses or duty free shops may be issued under section 24, including the security that may be required of operators of the warehouses or shops, the duration of the licences and the fees or the manner of determining fees, if any, to be paid for the licences;
(c) prescribing the circumstances in which licences for the operation of sufferance warehouses or duty free shops may be issued, amended, suspended, renewed, cancelled or reinstated;
(d) establishing standards for the operation of and the maintenance of the facilities of sufferance warehouses or duty free shops;
(e) prescribing the manner of acknowledging receipt of goods in sufferance warehouses or duty free shops;
(f) establishing the circumstances in which and the extent to which goods may be manipulated, unpacked, packed, altered or combined with other goods while in sufferance warehouses or duty free shops;

(g) prescribing facilities, equipment and personnel that must be provided at sufferance warehouses or duty free shops;
(h) prescribing the circumstances in which the operator of a sufferance warehouse may refuse goods that are brought to the warehouse for safe-keeping;
(i) regulating the transfer of ownership of goods in duty free shops;
(j) prescribing, with respect to goods, or classes of goods, that are offered for sale in a duty free shop, minimum proportions, by reference to quantity, value or other like standard, that must be of domestic origin;
(k) prescribing restrictions as to the classes of goods that may be received in sufferance warehouses;
(l) prescribing circumstances in which goods shall not be received in sufferance warehouses;
(m) regulating the provision of information by the operator of a duty free shop; and
(n) otherwise regulating the operation of sufferance warehouses or duty free shops.
R.S., 1985, c. 1 (2nd Supp.), s. 30;
1993, c. 25, s. 73;
1995, c. 41, s. 7.

Release

Release
31 Subject to section 19, no goods shall be removed from a customs office, sufferance warehouse, bonded warehouse or duty free shop by any person other than an officer in the performance of his or her duties under this or any other Act of Parliament unless the goods have been released by an officer or by any prescribed means.
R.S., 1985, c. 1 (2nd Supp.), s. 31;
2001, c. 25, s. 20.

Accounting and Payment of Duties

Accounting and payment of duties
32 (1) Subject to subsections (2) and (4) and any regulations made under subsection (6), and to section 33, no goods shall be released until
(a) they have been accounted for by the importer or owner thereof in the prescribed manner and, where they are to be accounted for in writing, in the prescribed form containing the prescribed information; and
(b) all duties thereon have been paid.
Release prior to accounting
(2) In prescribed circumstances and under prescribed conditions, goods may be released prior to the accounting required under subsection (1) if
(a) the importer or owner of the goods makes an interim accounting in the prescribed manner and form and containing the prescribed information, or in the form and containing the information that is satisfactory to the Minister; or
(b) the goods have been authorized by an officer or by any prescribed means for delivery to, and have been received at, the place of business of the importer, owner or consignee of the goods.
Accounting after release
(3) If goods are released under subsection (2), they shall be accounted for within the prescribed time and in the manner described in paragraph (1)(a) by, in the case of goods to which paragraph (2)(a) applies, the person who made the interim accounting under that paragraph in respect of the goods and, in the case of goods to which paragraph (2)(b) applies, by the importer or owner of the goods.
Release of goods
(4) In such circumstances, and under such conditions, as may be prescribed, goods imported by courier or as mail may be released prior to the accounting required under subsection (1) and prior to the payment of duties thereon.

Accounting and payment of duties
(5) Where goods are released under subsection (4),
(a) the person who is authorized under paragraph (6)(a) or subsection (7) to account for the goods shall, within the prescribed time, account for the goods in the manner described in paragraph (1)(a) and that person or the importer or owner of the goods shall, within the prescribed time, pay duties on the goods, or
(b) where there is no person authorized under paragraph (6)(a) or subsection (7) to account for the goods, the importer or owner of the goods shall, within the prescribed time, account for the goods in the manner described in paragraph (1)(a) and shall, within the prescribed time, pay duties on the goods.

Deemed accounting
(5.1) Except in prescribed circumstances, where the importer or owner of mail that has been released as mail under subsection (4) takes delivery of the mail, the mail shall be deemed to have been accounted for under subsection (5) at the time of its release.

Regulations
(6) The Governor in Council may make regulations
(a) specifying persons or classes of persons who are authorized to account for goods under this section in lieu of the importer or owner thereof and prescribing the circumstances in which and the conditions under which such persons or classes of persons are so authorized; and
(b) prescribing the circumstances in which goods may be released without any requirement of accounting.

Authorization to account
(7) The Minister or an officer designated by the President for the purposes of this subsection may authorize any person not resident in Canada to account for goods under this section, in such circumstances and under such conditions as may be prescribed, in lieu of the importer or owner of those goods.

R.S., 1985, c. 1 (2nd Supp.), s. 32;
1992, c. 28, s. 5;
1995, c. 41, s. 8;
2001, c. 25, s. 21;
2005, c. 38, s. 63.

Statistics
32.1 (1) Subject to this section, every person who accounts for goods under subsection 32(1), (3) or (5) shall, at the time of accounting, furnish an officer at a customs office with the statistical code for the goods determined by reference to the Coding System established pursuant to section 22.1 of the Statistics Act

Prescribed form
(2) The statistical code referred to in subsection (1) shall be furnished in the prescribed manner and in the prescribed form containing the prescribed information.

Regulations
(3) The Governor in Council may make regulations exempting persons or goods, or classes thereof, from the requirements of subsection (1) subject to such conditions, if any, as are specified in the regulations.

1988, c. 65, s. 68.

Correction to declaration of origin
32.2 (1) An importer or owner of goods for which preferential tariff treatment under a free trade agreement has been claimed or any person authorized to account for those goods under paragraph 32(6)(a) or subsection 32(7) shall, within ninety days after the importer, owner or person has reason to believe that a declaration of origin for those goods made under this Act is incorrect,
(a) make a correction to the declaration of origin in the prescribed manner and in the prescribed form containing the prescribed information; and
(b) pay any amount owing as duties as a result of the correction to the declaration of origin and any

interest owing or that may become owing on that amount.
(1.1) Corrections to other declarations
(2) Subject to regulations made under subsection (7), an importer or owner of goods or a person who is within a prescribed class of persons in relation to goods or is authorized under paragraph 32(6)(a) or subsection 32(7) to account for goods shall, within ninety days after the importer, owner or person has reason to believe that the declaration of origin (other than a declaration of origin referred to in subsection (1)), declaration of tariff classification or declaration of value for duty made under this Act for any of those goods is incorrect,
(a) make a correction to the declaration in the prescribed form and manner, with the prescribed information; and
(b) pay any amount owing as duties as a result of the correction to the declaration and any interest owing or that may become owing on that amount.
Correction treated as re-determination
(3) A correction made under this section is to be treated for the purposes of this Act as if it were a re-determination under paragraph 59(1)(a).
Four-year limit on correction obligation
(4) The obligation under this section to make a correction in respect of imported goods ends four years after the goods are accounted for under subsection 32(1), (3) or (5).
Correction not to result in refund
(5) This section does not apply to require or allow a correction that would result in a claim for a refund of duties.
Diversions
(6) The obligation under this section to make a correction to a declaration of tariff classification includes an obligation to correct a declaration of tariff classification that is rendered incorrect by a failure, after the goods are accounted for under subsection 32(1), (3) or (5) or, in the case of prescribed goods, after the goods are released without accounting, to comply with a condition imposed under a tariff item in the List of Tariff Provisions set out in the schedule to the Customs Tariff
Regulations
(7) The Governor in Council may make regulations prescribing the circumstances in which certain goods are exempt from the operation of subsection (6) and the classes of goods in respect of which, the length of time for which and the conditions under which the exemptions apply.
Duties
(8) If a declaration of tariff classification is rendered incorrect by a failure referred to in subsection (6), for the purposes of paragraph (2)(b), duties do not include duties or taxes levied under the Excise Act, 2001
Excise Tax Act
Special Import Measures Act
1993, c. 44, s. 82;
1996, c. 33, s. 29;
1997, c. 14, s. 36, c. 36, s. 152;
2001, c. 25, s. 22;
2002, c. 22, s. 333.
Diversion of goods used as ships' stores
32.3 If goods are removed or caused to be removed for use as ships' stores under paragraph 19(1)(c) or (2)(c), and the goods are subsequently diverted to another use, the person who diverted the goods shall, at the time of the diversion,
(a) report the diversion to an officer at a customs office;
(b) account for the goods in the prescribed manner and in the prescribed form containing the prescribed information; and
(c) pay as duties on the goods an amount equal to the amount of duties that would be payable on like goods imported in like condition at the time of the diversion.

2001, c. 25, s. 23.
Release prior to payment of duties
33 (1) In prescribed circumstances, goods may be released prior to the payment of duties levied on them.
Payment of duties
(2) If goods are released under this section, the person who accounted for the goods under subsection 32(2) or (3) shall pay the duties levied on them within the prescribed time.
Meaning of duties
(3) In subsection (2),
duties
(a) subsection 21.1(1) of the
Customs Tariff
(b) subsections 21.2(1) and (2) of the
Customs Tariff
R.S., 1985, c. 1 (2nd Supp.), s. 33;
1992, c. 28, s. 6;
2002, c. 22, s. 334.
33.1 Notice requiring accounting
33.2 The Minister or any officer designated by the President for the purposes of this section may, by notice served personally or by registered or certified mail, require any person to account, within such reasonable time as may be stipulated in the notice, in the manner described in paragraph 32(1)(a), for any goods as may be designated in the notice.
1992, c. 28, s. 7;
2005, c. 38, s. 64.
33.3 Interest
33.4 (1) Subject to subsection (3), any person who is liable to pay an amount of duties in respect of imported goods shall pay, in addition to the amount, interest at the specified rate for the period beginning on the first day after the day the person became liable to pay the amount and ending on the day the amount has been paid in full, calculated on the outstanding balance of the amount.
When duties deemed payable
(2) For the purposes of subsection (1), any duties in respect of goods payable under paragraph 59(3)(a) or 65(1)(a) of this Act or under the
Special Import Measures Act
Interest-free period
(3) If an amount of duties in respect of goods that is payable by a person under paragraph 59(3)(a) or 65(1)(a) in accordance with a determination, re-determination or further re-determination made under this Act is paid by the person or if an amount of duties in respect of goods that is payable under the
Special Import Measures Act
1992, c. 28, s. 7;
1994, c. 47, s. 70;
1995, c. 41, s. 9;
1997, c. 36, s. 154;
2001, c. 25, s. 26.
Notice requiring payment
33.5 The Minister or any officer designated by the President for the purposes of this section may, by notice served personally or by registered or certified mail, require any person to pay any amount owing as duties, within such reasonable time as may be stipulated in the notice, on any goods as may be designated in the notice.
1992, c. 28, s. 7;
2005, c. 38, s. 65.
33.6 Extension of time

33.7 (1) The Minister or any officer designated by the President for the purposes of this section may at any time extend in writing the time prescribed by the regulations made under this Part for the accounting of goods or the payment of any amount owing as duties.
Effect of extension for accounting
(2) Where the time within which a person must account for goods is extended under subsection (1),
(a) the goods shall be accounted for within the time as so extended;
(b) if the person accounts for the goods within the extended time, no penalty shall be imposed under section 109.1; and
(c) if the person fails to account for the goods within the time as so extended, the extension shall be deemed not to have been made.
Effect of extension for payment
(3) Where the time within which a person must pay any amount owing as duties is extended under subsection (1),
(a) that amount shall be paid within the time as so extended;
(b) if the person pays that amount within the time as so extended, subsection 33.4(1) shall apply in respect of that amount as if the time had not been so extended, but interest payable under that subsection in respect of that amount shall be computed at the prescribed rate rather than at the specified rate; and
(c) if the person fails to pay the amount within the time as so extended, the extension shall be deemed not to have been made.
1992, c. 28, s. 7;
2001, c. 25, s. 28;
2005, c. 38, s. 66.
33.8 34 Security and conditions of release
35 Except in such circumstances as may be prescribed, no goods shall be released under subsection 32(2) or (4) or section 33 until such deposits, bonds or other security as may be prescribed is given, and any goods that are released under those provisions shall be released subject to such terms and conditions as may be prescribed.
R.S., 1985, c. 1 (2nd Supp.), s. 35;
1995, c. 41, s. 11.

Marking of Goods

Requirement to comply with marking regulations
35.01 No person shall import goods that are required to be marked by any regulations made under section 19 of the
Customs Tariff
1993, c. 44, s. 83;
1997, c. 36, s. 155.
35.02 (1) Notice requiring marking or compliance
(2) The Minister or any officer designated by the President for the purposes of this section may, by notice served personally or by registered mail, require any person
(a) to mark imported goods in accordance with the regulations made under section 19 of the Customs Tariff
(b) to comply with section 35.01 in respect of any goods designated in the notice that will subsequently be imported by the person.
(3) Goods imported from a NAFTA country
(4) If a person imports goods of a prescribed class from a NAFTA country, that person is not liable to a penalty under section 109.1 unless
(a) the person has previously failed to comply with section 35.01 in respect of imported goods and has been given notice pursuant to subsection (2);
(b) the goods with respect to which there has been a failure to comply with section 35.01 or a notice

given pursuant to subsection (2) have been released without being marked in the manner referred to in section 35.01; or
(c) the imported goods have been marked in a deceptive manner so as to mislead another person as to the country or geographic area of origin of the goods.
(5) 1993, c. 44, s. 83;
1997, c. 36, s. 156;
2001, c. 25, s. 30;
2005, c. 38, s. 67.

Origin of Goods

Proof of origin
35.1 (1) Subject to any regulations made under subsection (4), proof of origin, in the prescribed form containing the prescribed information and containing or accompanied by the information, statements or proof required by any regulations made under subsection (4), shall be furnished in respect of all goods that are imported.
When furnished
(2) Proof of origin of goods shall be furnished under subsection (1) to an officer at such time and place and in such manner as may be prescribed.
Who furnishes
(3) Subject to any regulations made under subsection (4), proof of origin of goods shall be furnished under subsection (1) by the importer or owner thereof.
Regulations
(4) The Governor in Council, on the recommendation of the Minister and the Minister of Finance, may make regulations
(a) specifying persons or classes of persons who are authorized to furnish proof of origin of goods under subsection (1) in lieu of the importer or owner thereof and prescribing the circumstances in which and the conditions, if any, under which such persons or classes of persons are so authorized;
(b) specifying information required to be contained in, or to accompany, the prescribed proof of origin form in addition to the prescribed information and specifying any statements or proof required to be contained therein or to accompany that form; and
(c) exempting persons or goods, or classes thereof, from the requirements of subsection (1) subject to such conditions, if any, as are specified in the regulations.
Denial or withdrawal of preferential tariff treatment
(5) Preferential tariff treatment under a free trade agreement may be denied or withdrawn in respect of goods for which that treatment is claimed if the importer, owner or other person required to furnish proof of origin of the goods under this section fails to comply with any provision of this Act or the
Customs Tariff
(6) 1988, c. 65, s. 69;
1992, c. 28, s. 9;
1993, c. 44, s. 84;
1996, c. 33, s. 30;
1997, c. 14, s. 37;
2012, c. 18, s. 25(F).

Abandoned Goods

Abandonment of goods to the Crown
36 (1) The owner of goods that have been imported but have not been released may, with the authorization of an officer and subject to the conditions set out in subsection (2), abandon the goods to Her Majesty in right of Canada.

Conditions of abandonment
(2) Any person who abandons goods to Her Majesty under subsection (1) is liable for all reasonable expenses incurred by Her Majesty in the disposal of the goods where they are disposed of otherwise than by sale.

Unclaimed Goods

Unclaimed goods
37 (1) Goods, other than goods of a prescribed class, that have not been removed from a customs office, sufferance warehouse or duty free shop within such period of time as may be prescribed may be deposited by an officer in a place of safe-keeping designated by the Minister for that purpose.
Unclaimed goods in a bonded warehouse
(2) Goods, other than goods of a class prescribed by regulations made under subparagraph 99(f)(xii) of the
Customs Tariff
Extension of prescribed period
(3) The Minister may extend any period of time prescribed pursuant to subsection (1) or (2) in respect of any particular goods.
Deeming provision
(4) A place of safe-keeping referred to in this section shall, for the purposes of this Act, be deemed to be a customs office.
R.S., 1985, c. 1 (2nd Supp.), s. 37;
1993, c. 25, s. 74;
1995, c. 41, s. 12;
1997, c. 36, s. 157.
Risk and storage charges
38 (1) Goods that are deposited in a place of safe-keeping under section 37 shall be kept there at the risk of the owner and importer of those goods, and the owner and importer are jointly and severally, or solidarily, liable for any storage charges that may be prescribed and any expenses incurred in moving the goods from the customs office, sufferance warehouse, bonded warehouse or duty free shop to the place of safe-keeping.
No removal until expenses paid
(2) No goods shall be removed by any person other than an officer from a place of safe-keeping referred to in section 37 until the charges and expenses referred to in subsection (1) have been paid.
1985, c. 1 (2nd Supp.), s. 38;
2004, c. 25, s. 121(E).
Unclaimed goods forfeit
39 (1) Goods that have not been removed from a place of safe-keeping referred to in section 37 within such period of time after they were deposited therein as may be prescribed are, at the termination of that period of time, forfeit.
Expenses of disposal
(2) The importer of goods that are forfeit under subsection (1) and the owner of those goods at the time of forfeiture are jointly and severally, or solidarily, liable for all reasonable expenses incurred by Her Majesty in right of Canada in the disposal of the goods if they are disposed of otherwise than by sale.
1985, c. 1 (2nd Supp.), s. 39;
2004, c. 25, s. 122(E).

Goods of a Prescribed Class

Goods forfeit if not removed
39.1 (1) Goods of a prescribed class that have not been removed from a customs office, sufferance

warehouse or duty free shop within such period of time as may be prescribed are, at the end of that period of time, forfeit.

Goods in bonded warehouse forfeit if not removed

(2) Goods of a class prescribed by regulations made under subparagraph 99(f)(xii) of the Customs Tariff

1993, c. 25, s. 75;
1995, c. 41, s. 13;
1997, c. 36, s. 158.

Records

Importers' records

40 (1) Every person who imports goods or causes goods to be imported for sale or for any industrial, occupational, commercial, institutional or other like use or any other use that may be prescribed shall keep at the person's place of business in Canada or at any other place that may be designated by the Minister any records in respect of those goods in any manner and for any period of time that may be prescribed and shall, where an officer so requests, make them available to the officer, within the time specified by the officer, and answer truthfully any questions asked by the officer in respect of the records.

Minister's request

(2) If, in the opinion of the Minister, a person has not kept records in accordance with subsection (1), the Minister may request that person to comply with that subsection in respect of the records.

Requirement to keep records

(3) The following persons shall keep at their place of business or at any other place that may be designated by the Minister the prescribed records with respect to the prescribed goods, in the manner and for the period that may be prescribed, and shall, where an officer requests, make them available to the officer, within the time specified by the officer, and answer truthfully any questions asked by the officer in respect of the records:

(a) a person who is granted a licence under section 24;
(b) a person who receives goods authorized for delivery to the person's place of business in the circumstances set out in paragraph 32(2)(b);
(c) a person who is authorized under paragraph 32(6)(a) or subsection 32(7) to account for goods;
(d) a person who is granted a certificate under section 90 of the Customs Tariff
(e) a person who is granted a licence under section 91 of that Act.

Minister's request

(4) Where, in the opinion of the Minister, a person has not kept records in respect of goods in accordance with subsection (3), the Minister may request that person to comply with that subsection in respect of the goods.

R.S., 1985, c. 1 (2nd Supp.), s. 40;
1992, c. 28, s. 10;
1993, c. 44, s. 85;
1995, c. 41, s. 15;
1997, c. 36, s. 159;
2001, c. 25, s. 31.

Detention of goods

41 (1) Any goods imported by or on behalf of a person to whom a request is made under subsection 40(2) at any time after the request is made may be detained by an officer at the expense of that person until the request is complied with.

Disposition of detained goods

(2) Goods that are detained under subsection (1) may be deposited in a place of safe-keeping in accordance with subsection 37(1) as if they were unclaimed and may be dealt with thereafter under

sections 37 to 39.

Definition of
dwelling-house

42 (1) In this section,

dwelling-house

(a) a building within the curtilage of a dwelling-house that is connected to it by a doorway or by a covered and enclosed passageway; and

(b) a unit that is designed to be mobile and to be used as a permanent or temporary residence and that is being used as such a residence.

Inspections

(2) An officer, or an officer within a class of officers, designated by the President for the purposes of this section, may at all reasonable times, for any purpose related to the administration or enforcement of this Act,

(a) inspect, audit or examine any record of a person that relates or may relate to the information that is or should be in the records of the person or to any amount paid or payable under this Act;

(b) examine property in an inventory of a person and any property or process of, or matter relating to, the person, an examination of which may assist the officer in determining the accuracy of the inventory of the person or in ascertaining the information that is or should be in the records of the person or any amount paid or payable by the person under this Act;

(c) subject to subsection (3), enter any premises or place where any business is carried on, any property is kept, anything is done in connection with any business or any records are or should be kept; and

(d) require the owner or manager of the property or business and any other person on the premises or place to give the officer all reasonable assistance and to answer truthfully any question, and, for that purpose, require the owner, manager or other person designated by the owner or manager to attend at the premises or place with the officer.

Prior authorization

(3) If any premises or place referred to in paragraph (2)(c) is a dwelling-house, an officer may not enter that dwelling-house without the consent of the occupant except under the authority of a warrant under subsection (4).

Warrant

(4) On

(a) there are reasonable grounds to believe that the dwelling-house is a premises or place referred to in paragraph (2)(c);

(b) entry into the dwelling-house is necessary; and

(c) entry into the dwelling-house has been, or there are reasonable grounds to believe that entry into the dwelling-house will be, refused.

Other access to document

(5) If the judge is not satisfied that entry into that dwelling-house is necessary for any purpose relating to the administration or enforcement of this Act but is satisfied that access to a document or property that is or should be kept in the dwelling-house has been or may be expected to be refused, the judge may

(a) order the occupant of the dwelling-house to provide the officer with reasonable access to any document or property; and

(b) make any other order that is appropriate in the circumstances to carry out the purposes of this Act.

R.S., 1985, c. 1 (2nd Supp.), s. 42;
2001, c. 25, s. 32;
2005, c. 38, s. 68.

Verifications

Methods of verification
42.01 An officer, or an officer within a class of officers, designated by the President for the purposes of this section may conduct a verification of origin (other than a verification of origin referred to in section 42.1), verification of tariff classification or verification of value for duty in respect of imported goods in the manner that is prescribed and may for that purpose at all reasonable times enter any prescribed premises.
1997, c. 36, s. 160;
2001, c. 25, s. 33;
2005, c. 38, s. 69.

Verifications under a Free Trade Agreement

Conduct of Verification

Methods of verification
42.1 (1) Any officer, or any officer within a class of officers, designated by the President for the purposes of this section, or any person, or any person within a class of persons, designated by the President to act on behalf of such an officer, may, subject to the prescribed conditions,
(a) conduct a verification of origin of goods for which preferential tariff treatment under a free trade agreement, other than a free trade agreement referred to in subsection (1.1), is claimed
(i) by entering any prescribed premises or place at any reasonable time, or
(ii) in the prescribed manner; or
(b) enter any prescribed premises or place at any reasonable time to verify the amount, if any, of
(i) a relief under section 89 of the
Customs Tariff
(ii) a drawback under section 113 of the
Customs Tariff
Method of verification — certain agreements
(1.1) Any officer, or any officer within a class of officers, designated by the President for the purposes of this section, or any person, or any person within a class of persons, designated by the President to act on behalf of such an officer, may, subject to any prescribed conditions, conduct any of the following:
(a) a verification of origin of goods for which preferential tariff treatment under CEFTA is claimed, by requesting in writing that the customs administration of the EFTA state of export conduct a verification and provide an opinion as to whether the goods are originating within the meaning of Annex C of CEFTA;
(b) a verification of origin of goods for which preferential tariff treatment under CUFTA is claimed, by requesting in writing that the customs administration of Ukraine conduct a verification and provide a written report as to whether the goods are originating within the meaning of Chapter 3 of CUFTA;
(c) a verification of origin of goods for which preferential tariff treatment under CETA is claimed, by requesting in writing that the customs administration of the EU country or other CETA beneficiary of export conduct a verification and provide a written report as to whether the goods are originating within the meaning of the Protocol on Rules of Origin and Origin Procedures of CETA.
Withdrawal of preferential tariff treatment
(2) If an exporter or producer of goods that are subject to a verification of origin under paragraph (1)(a) fails to comply with the prescribed requirements or, in the case of a verification of origin under subparagraph (1)(a)(i), does not consent to the verification of origin in the prescribed manner and within the prescribed time, preferential tariff treatment under a free trade agreement, other than a free trade agreement referred to in subsection (1.1), may be denied or withdrawn from the goods.
Withdrawal of preferential tariff treatment under CEFTA
(3) Preferential tariff treatment under a free trade agreement referred to in subsection (1.1) may be

denied or withdrawn from the goods in any of the following circumstances:
(a) in the case of CEFTA, if the EFTA state of export fails to conduct a verification or provide an opinion as to whether the goods are originating;
(a.1) in the case of CUFTA, if Ukraine fails to conduct a verification or provide a written report as to whether the goods are originating;
(a.2) in the case of CETA, if the EU country or other CETA beneficiary of export fails to conduct a verification or provide a written report as to whether the goods are originating;
(b) if an officer or other person designated under subsection (1.1) is unable to determine whether the goods are originating; or
(c) in any other prescribed circumstances.
1993, c. 44, s. 86;
1995, c. 41, s. 16;
1997, c. 14, s. 38, c. 36, s. 161;
2005, c. 38, s. 70;
2009, c. 6, s. 24;
2017, c. 6, s. 83, c. 8, ss. 21, 43.

Statement of Origin

Statement of origin

42.2 (1) On completion of a verification of origin under paragraph 42.1(1)(a), an officer designated under subsection 42.1(1) shall provide the exporter or producer whose goods are subject to the verification of origin with a statement as to whether the goods are eligible, under the
Customs Tariff

Basis of statement

(2) A statement referred to in subsection (1) must include any findings of fact or law on which it was based.
1993, c. 44, s. 86;
1997, c. 14, s. 38, c. 36, s. 162;
2012, c. 18, s. 26(F).

Effective Date of Re-determination of Origin

Definition of
customs administration
42.3 (1) In this section,
customs administration

Effective date of redetermination or further redetermination of origin of goods

(2) Subject to subsection (4), a redetermination or further redetermination of origin does not take effect until notice of it is given to the importer of the goods and any person who completed and signed a Certificate of Origin for the goods if the result of the redetermination or further redetermination of origin made under subsection 59(1) in respect of goods for which preferential tariff treatment under NAFTA, CCFTA, CCRFTA or CHFTA is claimed and that are the subject of a verification of origin under this Act is that
(a) the goods are not eligible for that preferential tariff treatment on the basis of the tariff classification or value of one or more materials used in their production; and
(b) that tariff classification or value differs from the tariff classification or value applied to those materials by the NAFTA country from which the goods were exported, from Chile, from Costa Rica or from Honduras, as the case may be.

Limitation

(3) A redetermination or further redetermination of origin referred to in subsection (2) shall not be applied to goods imported before the date on which the notice was given if the customs

administration of the NAFTA country from which the goods were exported, of Chile, of Costa Rica or of Honduras, as the case may be, has, before that date,

(a) given an advance ruling under Article 509 of NAFTA, Article E-09 of CCFTA, Article V.9 of CCRFTA, paragraph 1 of Article 5.10 or paragraph 11 of Article 6.2 of CHFTA as the case may be, or given another ruling referred to in paragraph 12 of Article 506 of NAFTA, paragraph 12 of Article E-06 of CCFTA, paragraph 15 of Article V.6 of CCRFTA, or paragraph 15 of Article 5.7 of CHFTA, as the case may be, on the tariff classification or value of the materials referred to in subsection (2); or

(b) given consistent treatment with respect to the tariff classification or value of the materials referred to in subsection (2) on their importation into the NAFTA country, Chile, Costa Rica or Honduras, as the case may be.

Postponement of effective date

(4) The date on which a redetermination or further redetermination of origin referred to in subsection (2) takes effect shall be postponed for a period not exceeding ninety days if the importer of the goods that are the subject of the redetermination or further redetermination or any person who completed and signed a Certificate of Origin for the goods establishes to the satisfaction of the Minister that the importer or the person, as the case may be, has relied in good faith, to the detriment of the importer or person, on the tariff classification or value applied to the materials referred to in that subsection by the customs administration of the NAFTA country from which the goods were exported, of Chile, Costa Rica or of Honduras, as the case may be.

Effect of detrimental reliance under CEFTA

(5) If an exporter of goods from an EFTA state demonstrates, to the satisfaction of the Minister, that it has relied, in good faith and to its detriment, on a ruling made by the Agency or the customs administration of an EFTA state with respect to the tariff classification or value of a non-originating material used in the production of goods, a redetermination of origin by the Agency in respect of goods for which preferential tariff treatment under CEFTA is claimed shall apply only to importations of the goods made after the date of the redetermination.

1993, c. 44, s. 86;
1997, c. 14, s. 38, c. 36, s. 163;
2001, c. 25, s. 34(F), c. 28, s. 27;
2009, c. 6, s. 25;
2014, c. 14, s. 24.

Denial or Withdrawal of Benefit of Preferential Tariff Treatment Under Certain Free Trade Agreements

Definition of
identical goods
42.4 (1) In this section,
identical goods

Denial or withdrawal of benefit — specified countries

(2) Notwithstanding section 24 of the
Customs Tariff
1993, c. 44, s. 86;
1997, c. 14, s. 38, c. 36, s. 164;
2001, c. 28, s. 27;
2009, c. 16, s. 32;
2010, c. 4, s. 26;
2012, c. 18, s. 27.
42.5 and 42.6

Production of Documents

Production of records
43 (1) The Minister may, for any purpose related to the administration or enforcement of this Act, including the collection of any amount owing under this Act by any person, by notice served personally or sent by registered or certified mail, require any person to provide any record at a place specified by the Minister and within any reasonable time that may be stipulated in the notice.
Compliance
(2) Any person who is required to provide any records, books, letters, accounts, invoices, statements or other documents or information under subsection (1) shall, notwithstanding any other law to the contrary but subject to subsection (3), do so as required.
Application of section 232 of the
Income Tax Act
(3) The definitions
lawyer
solicitor-client privilege
Income Tax Act
R.S., 1985, c. 1 (2nd Supp.), s. 43;
2000, c. 30, s. 160;
2001, c. 25, s. 35.

Advance Rulings

Advance rulings
43.1 (1) Any officer, or any officer within a class of officers, designated by the President for the purposes of this section shall, before goods are imported, on application by any member of a prescribed class that is made within the prescribed time, in the prescribed manner and in the prescribed form containing the prescribed information, give an advance ruling with respect to
(a) whether the goods qualify as originating goods and are entitled to the benefit of preferential tariff treatment under a free trade agreement;
(b) in the case of goods exported from a country or territory set out in column 1 of Part 3 of the schedule, any matter, other than those referred to in paragraphs (a) and (c), concerning those goods that is set out in the provision set out in column 2; and
(c) the tariff classification of the goods.
Regulations
(2) The Governor in Council may make regulations respecting advance rulings, including regulations respecting
(a) the application of an advance ruling;
(b) the modification or revocation of an advance ruling, including whether the modification or revocation applies retroactively;
(c) the authority to request supplementary information in respect of an application for an advance ruling; and
(d) the circumstances in which the issuance of advance rulings may be declined or postponed.
1993, c. 44, s. 87;
1996, c. 33, s. 33;
1997, c. 14, s. 39;
2001, c. 25, s. 36, c. 28, s. 28;
2004, c. 16, s. 6(F);
2005, c. 38, s. 71;
2009, c. 6, s. 26, c. 16, ss. 33, 56;
2010, c. 4, s. 27;
2012, c. 18, s. 28.

PART III

PART III
Calculation of Duty

Duties Based on Percentage Rates

Valuation for Duty

44 If duties, other than duties or taxes levied under the
Excise Act, 2001
Excise Tax Act
R.S., 1985, c. 1 (2nd Supp.), s. 44;
2002, c. 22, s. 335.

Interpretation

Definitions
45 (1) In this section and sections 46 to 55,
computed value
country of export
deductive value
goods of the same class or kind
(a) are within a group or range of imported goods produced by a particular industry or industry sector that includes identical goods and similar goods in relation to the goods being appraised, and
(b) for the purposes of
(i) section 51, were produced in any country and exported from any country, and
(ii) section 52, were produced in and exported from the same country as the country in and from which the goods being appraised were produced and exported;
identical goods
(a) are the same in all respects, including physical characteristics, quality and reputation, as the goods being appraised, except for minor differences in appearance that do not affect the value of the goods,
(b) were produced in the same country as the country in which the goods being appraised were produced, and
(c) were produced by or on behalf of the person by or on behalf of whom the goods being appraised were produced,
but does not include imported goods where engineering, development work, art work, design work, plans or sketches undertaken in Canada were supplied, directly or indirectly, by the purchaser of those imported goods free of charge or at a reduced cost for use in connection with the production and sale for export of those imported goods;
price paid or payable
produce
purchaser in Canada
similar goods
(a) closely resemble the goods being appraised in respect of their component materials and characteristics,
(b) are capable of performing the same functions as, and of being commercially interchangeable with, the goods being appraised,
(c) were produced in the same country as the country in which the goods being appraised were produced, and

(d) were produced by or on behalf of the person by or on behalf of whom the goods being appraised were produced,
but does not include imported goods where engineering, development work, art work, design work, plans or sketches undertaken in Canada were supplied, directly or indirectly, by the purchaser of those imported goods free of charge or at a reduced cost for use in connection with the production and sale for export of those imported goods;
sufficient information
transaction value

Goods deemed to be identical goods or similar goods
(2) For the purposes of this section and sections 46 to 55, where there are no identical goods or similar goods, as the case may be, in relation to goods being appraised but there are goods that would be identical goods or similar goods, as the case may be, if they were produced by or on behalf of the person by or on behalf of whom the goods being appraised were produced, those goods shall be deemed to be identical goods or similar goods, as the case may be.

Related persons
(3) For the purposes of sections 46 to 55, persons are related to each other if
(a) they are individuals connected by blood relationship, marriage, common-law partnership or adoption within the meaning of subsection 251(6) of the
Income Tax Act
(b) one is an officer or director of the other;
(c) each such person is an officer or director of the same two corporations, associations, partnerships or other organizations;
(d) they are partners;
(e) one is the employer of the other;
(f) they directly or indirectly control or are controlled by the same person;
(g) one directly or indirectly controls or is controlled by the other;
(h) any other person directly or indirectly owns, holds or controls five per cent or more of the outstanding voting stock or shares of each such person; or
(i) one directly or indirectly owns, holds or controls five per cent or more of the outstanding voting stock or shares of the other.
R.S., 1985, c. 1 (2nd Supp.), s. 45;
1995, c. 41, s. 17;
2000, c. 12, s. 96.

Determination of Value for Duty

Determination of value for duty
46 The value for duty of imported goods shall be determined in accordance with sections 47 to 55.

Order of Consideration of Methods of Valuation

Primary basis of appraisal
47 (1) The value for duty of goods shall be appraised on the basis of the transaction value of the goods in accordance with the conditions set out in section 48.
Subsidiary bases of appraisal
(2) Where the value for duty of goods is not appraised in accordance with subsection (1), it shall be appraised on the basis of the first of the following values, considered in the order set out herein, that can be determined in respect of the goods and that can, under sections 49 to 52, be the basis on which the value for duty of the goods is appraised:
(a) the transaction value of identical goods that meets the requirements set out in section 49;
(b) the transaction value of similar goods that meets the requirements set out in section 50;
(c) the deductive value of the goods; and

(d) the computed value of the goods.
Request of importer
(3) Notwithstanding subsection (2), on the written request of the importer of any goods being appraised made prior to the commencement of the appraisal of those goods, the order of consideration of the values referred to in paragraphs (2)(c) and (d) shall be reversed.
Residual basis of appraisal
(4) Where the value for duty of goods is not appraised on the basis of any of the values referred to in paragraphs (2)(a) to (d), the value for duty of those goods shall be appraised under section 53.

Transaction Value of the Goods

Transaction value as primary basis of appraisal
48 (1) Subject to subsections (6) and (7), the value for duty of goods is the transaction value of the goods if the goods are sold for export to Canada to a purchaser in Canada and the price paid or payable for the goods can be determined and if
(a) there are no restrictions respecting the disposition or use of the goods by the purchaser thereof, other than restrictions that
(i) are imposed by law,
(ii) limit the geographical area in which the goods may be resold, or
(iii) do not substantially affect the value of the goods;
(b) the sale of the goods by the vendor to the purchaser or the price paid or payable for the goods is not subject to some condition or consideration, with respect to the goods, in respect of which a value cannot be determined;
(c) when any part of the proceeds of any subsequent resale, disposal or use of the goods by the purchaser is to accrue, directly or indirectly, to the vendor, the price paid or payable for the goods includes the value of that part of the proceeds or the price is adjusted in accordance with paragraph (5)(a); and
(d) the purchaser and the vendor of the goods are not related to each other at the time the goods are sold for export or, where the purchaser and the vendor are related to each other at that time,
(i) their relationship did not influence the price paid or payable for the goods, or
(ii) the importer of the goods demonstrates that the transaction value of the goods meets the requirement set out in subsection (3).
Procedure in application of paragraph (1)(d)
(2) In the application of paragraph (1)(d), where the purchaser and the vendor of goods being appraised are related to each other at the time the goods are sold for export and the officer who is appraising the value for duty of the goods has grounds to believe that the requirement set out in subparagraph (1)(d)(i) is not met, the officer shall notify the importer of the goods of such grounds and, on the written request of the importer, the notification shall be in writing.
Requirement for accepting transaction value where purchaser and vendor related
(3) For the purposes of subparagraph (1)(d)(ii), the transaction value of goods being appraised shall, taking into consideration any relevant factors including, without limiting the generality of the foregoing, such factors and differences as may be prescribed, closely approximate one of the following values that is in respect of identical goods or similar goods exported at the same or substantially the same time as the goods being appraised and is the value for duty of the goods to which it relates:
(a) the transaction value of identical goods or similar goods in a sale of those goods for export to Canada between a vendor and purchaser who are not related to each other at the time of the sale;
(b) the deductive value of identical goods or similar goods; or
(c) the computed value of identical goods or similar goods.
Determination of transaction value
(4) The transaction value of goods shall be determined by ascertaining the price paid or payable for the goods when the goods are sold for export to Canada and adjusting the price paid or payable in

accordance with subsection (5).
Adjustment of price paid or payable
(5) The price paid or payable in the sale of goods for export to Canada shall be adjusted
(a) by adding thereto amounts, to the extent that each such amount is not already included in the price paid or payable for the goods, equal to
(i) commissions and brokerage in respect of the goods incurred by the purchaser thereof, other than fees paid or payable by the purchaser to his agent for the service of representing the purchaser abroad in respect of the sale,
(ii) the packing costs and charges incurred by the purchaser in respect of the goods, including the cost of cartons, cases and other containers and coverings that are treated for customs purposes as being part of the imported goods and all expenses of packing incident to placing the goods in the condition in which they are shipped to Canada,
(iii) the value of any of the following goods and services, determined in the manner prescribed, that are supplied, directly or indirectly, by the purchaser of the goods free of charge or at a reduced cost for use in connection with the production and sale for export of the imported goods, apportioned to the imported goods in a reasonable manner and in accordance with generally accepted accounting principles:
(A) materials, components, parts and other goods incorporated in the imported goods,
(B) tools, dies, moulds and other goods utilized in the production of the imported goods,
(C) any materials consumed in the production of the imported goods, and
(D) engineering, development work, art work, design work, plans and sketches undertaken elsewhere than in Canada and necessary for the production of the imported goods,
(iv) royalties and licence fees, including payments for patents, trade-marks and copyrights, in respect of the goods that the purchaser of the goods must pay, directly or indirectly, as a condition of the sale of the goods for export to Canada, exclusive of charges for the right to reproduce the goods in Canada,
(v) the value of any part of the proceeds of any subsequent resale, disposal or use of the goods by the purchaser thereof that accrues or is to accrue, directly or indirectly, to the vendor, and
(vi) the cost of transportation of, the loading, unloading and handling charges and other charges and expenses associated with the transportation of, and the cost of insurance relating to the transportation of, the goods to the place within the country of export from which the goods are shipped directly to Canada;
(b) by deducting therefrom amounts, to the extent that each such amount is included in the price paid or payable for the goods, equal to
(i) the cost of transportation of, the loading, unloading and handling charges and other charges and expenses associated with the transportation of, and the cost of insurance relating to the transportation of, the goods from the place within the country of export from which the goods are shipped directly to Canada, and
(ii) any of the following costs, charges or expenses if the cost, charge or expense is identified separately from the price paid or payable for the goods:
(A) any reasonable cost, charge or expense that is incurred for the construction, erection, assembly or maintenance of, or technical assistance provided in respect of, the goods after the goods are imported, and
(B) any duties and taxes paid or payable by reason of the importation of the goods or sale of the goods in Canada, including, without limiting the generality of the foregoing, any duties or taxes levied on the goods under the
Customs Tariff
Excise Act, 2001
Excise Tax Act
Special Import Measures Act
(c) by disregarding any rebate of, or other decrease in, the price paid or payable for the goods that is effected after the goods are imported.

Effect of absence of sufficient information
(6) Where there is not sufficient information to determine any of the amounts required to be added to the price paid or payable in respect of any goods being appraised, the value for duty of the goods shall not be appraised under this section.
Where information inaccurate
(7) Where an officer who is appraising the value for duty of goods believes on reasonable grounds that the information submitted in support of the transaction value of the goods as determined under subsection (4) is inaccurate, the officer shall determine, in accordance with the prescribed procedure, that the value for duty of the goods shall not be appraised under this section.
R.S., 1985, c. 1 (2nd Supp.), s. 48;
1994, c. 47, s. 71;
1995, c. 41, s. 18;
2002, c. 22, s. 336;
2009, c. 10, s. 7.

Transaction Value of Identical Goods

Transaction value of identical goods as value for duty
49 (1) Subject to subsections (2) to (5), where the value for duty of goods is not appraised under section 48, the value for duty of the goods is, if it can be determined, the transaction value of identical goods, in a sale of those goods for export to Canada, if that transaction value is the value for duty of the identical goods and the identical goods were exported at the same or substantially the same time as the goods being appraised and were sold under the following conditions:
(a) at the same or substantially the same trade level as the goods being appraised; and
(b) in the same or substantially the same quantities as the goods being appraised.
Where identical goods sold under different conditions
(2) Where the value for duty of goods being appraised cannot be determined under subsection (1) because identical goods were not sold under the conditions described in paragraphs (1)(a) and (b), there shall be substituted therefor, in the application of subsection (1), identical goods sold under any of the following conditions:
(a) at the same or substantially the same trade level as the goods being appraised but in different quantities;
(b) at a trade level different from that of the goods being appraised but in the same or substantially the same quantities; or
(c) at a trade level different from that of the goods being appraised and in different quantities.
Adjustment of transaction value of identical goods
(3) For the purposes of determining the value for duty of goods being appraised under subsection (1), the transaction value of identical goods shall be adjusted by adding thereto or deducting therefrom, as the case may be, amounts to account for
(a) commercially significant differences between the costs, charges and expenses referred to in subparagraph 48(5)(a)(vi) in respect of the identical goods and those costs, charges and expenses in respect of the goods being appraised that are attributable to differences in distances and modes of transport; and
(b) if the transaction value is in respect of identical goods sold under the conditions described in any of paragraphs (2)(a) to (c), differences in the trade levels of the identical goods and the goods being appraised or the quantities in which the identical goods were sold and the goods being appraised were imported or both, as the case may be.
Effect of absence of sufficient information
(4) Where there is not sufficient information to determine any amount referred to in subsection (3) or the adjustment therefor in relation to the transaction value of identical goods, the value for duty of the goods being appraised shall not be appraised on the basis of that transaction value under this section.

Selection of lowest transaction value of identical goods
(5) Where, in relation to goods being appraised, there are two or more transaction values of identical goods that meet all the requirements set out in subsections (1) and (3) or, where there is no such transaction value but there are two or more transaction values of identical goods sold under the conditions described in any of paragraphs (2)(a) to (c) that meet all the requirements set out in this section that are applicable by virtue of subsection (2), the value for duty of the goods being appraised shall be determined on the basis of the lowest such transaction value.
R.S., 1985, c. 1 (2nd Supp.), s. 49;
2009, c. 10, s. 8.

Transaction Value of Similar Goods

Transaction value of similar goods as value for duty
50 (1) Subject to subsections (2) and 49(2) to (5), where the value for duty of goods is not appraised under section 48 or 49, the value for duty of the goods is, if it can be determined, the transaction value of similar goods, in a sale of those goods for export to Canada, if that transaction value is the value for duty of the similar goods and the similar goods were exported at the same or substantially the same time as the goods being appraised and were sold under the following conditions:
(a) at the same or substantially the same trade level as the goods being appraised; and
(b) in the same or substantially the same quantities as the goods being appraised.
Application of section 49
(2) Subsections 49(2) to (5) apply to this section in respect of similar goods and wherever in those subsections the expression "identical goods" is referred to, there shall be substituted therefor the expression "similar goods".
R.S., 1985, c. 1 (2nd Supp.), s. 50;
2009, c. 10, s. 9.

Deductive Value

Deductive value as value for duty
51 (1) Subject to subsections (5) and 47(3), where the value for duty of goods is not appraised under sections 48 to 50, the value for duty of the goods is the deductive value of the goods if it can be determined.
Determination of deductive value
(2) The deductive value of goods being appraised is
(a) where the goods being appraised, identical goods or similar goods are sold in Canada in the condition in which they were imported at the same or substantially the same time as the time of importation of the goods being appraised, the price per unit, determined in accordance with subsection (3) and adjusted in accordance with subsection (4), at which the greatest number of units of the goods being appraised, identical goods or similar goods are so sold;
(b) where the goods being appraised, identical goods or similar goods are not sold in Canada in the circumstances described in paragraph (a) but are sold in Canada in the condition in which they were imported before the expiration of ninety days after the time of importation of the goods being appraised, the price per unit, determined in accordance with subsection (3) and adjusted in accordance with subsection (4), at which the greatest number of units of the goods being appraised, identical goods or similar goods are so sold at the earliest date after the time of importation of the goods being appraised; or
(c) where the goods being appraised, identical goods or similar goods are not sold in Canada in the circumstances described in paragraph (a) or (b) but the goods being appraised, after being assembled, packaged or further processed in Canada, are sold in Canada before the expiration of one hundred and eighty days after the time of importation thereof and the importer of the goods being appraised requests that this paragraph be applied in the determination of the value for duty of those goods, the

price per unit, determined in accordance with subsection (3) and adjusted in accordance with subsection (4), at which the greatest number of units of the goods being appraised are so sold.

Price per unit

(3) For the purposes of subsection (2), the price per unit, in respect of goods being appraised, identical goods or similar goods, shall be determined by ascertaining the unit price, in respect of sales of the goods at the first trade level after importation thereof to persons who

(a) are not related to the persons from whom they buy the goods at the time the goods are sold to them, and

(b) have not supplied, directly or indirectly, free of charge or at a reduced cost for use in connection with the production and sale for export of the goods any of the goods or services referred to in subparagraph 48(5)(a)(iii),

at which the greatest number of units of the goods is sold where, in the opinion of the Minister or any person authorized by him, a sufficient number of such sales have been made to permit a determination of the price per unit of the goods.

Adjustment of price per unit

(4) For the purposes of subsection (2), the price per unit, in respect of goods being appraised, identical goods or similar goods, shall be adjusted by deducting therefrom an amount equal to the aggregate of

(a) an amount, determined in the manner prescribed, equal to

(i) the amount of commission generally earned on a unit basis, or

(ii) the amount for profit and general expenses, including all costs of marketing the goods, considered together as a whole, that is generally reflected on a unit basis

in connection with sales in Canada of goods of the same class or kind as those goods,

(b) the costs, charges and expenses in respect of the transportation and insurance of the goods within Canada and the costs, charges and expenses associated therewith that are generally incurred in connection with sales in Canada of the goods being appraised, identical goods or similar goods, to the extent that an amount for such costs, charges and expenses is not deducted in respect of general expenses under paragraph (a),

(c) the costs, charges and expenses referred to in subparagraph 48(5)(b)(i), incurred in respect of the goods, to the extent that an amount for such costs, charges and expenses is not deducted in respect of general expenses under paragraph (a),

(d) any duties and taxes referred to in clause 48(5)(b)(ii)(B) in respect of the goods, to the extent that an amount for such duties and taxes is not deducted in respect of general expenses under paragraph (a), and

(e) where paragraph (2)(c) applies, the amount of the value added to the goods that is attributable to the assembly, packaging or further processing in Canada of the goods.

Rejection of deductive value

(5) Where there is not sufficient information to determine an amount referred to in paragraph (4)(e) in respect of any goods being appraised, the value for duty of the goods shall not be appraised under paragraph (2)(c).

Definition of

time of importation

(6) In this section,

time of importation

(a) in respect of goods other than those to which paragraph 32(2)(b) applies, the date on which an officer authorizes the release of the goods under this Act or the date on which their release is authorized by any prescribed means; and

(b) in respect of goods to which paragraph 32(2)(b) applies, the date on which the goods are received at the place of business of the importer, owner or consignee.

R.S., 1985, c. 1 (2nd Supp.), s. 51;
2001, c. 25, s. 37.

Computed Value

Computed value as value for duty
52 (1) Subject to subsection 47(3), where the value for duty of goods is not appraised under sections 48 to 51, the value for duty of the goods is the computed value of the goods if it can be determined.
Determination of computed value
(2) The computed value of goods being appraised is the aggregate of amounts equal to
(a) subject to subsection (3), the costs, charges and expenses incurred in respect of, or the value of,
(i) materials employed in producing the goods being appraised, and
(ii) the production or other processing of the goods being appraised,
determined in the manner prescribed; and
(b) the amount, determined in the manner prescribed, for profit and general expenses considered together as a whole, that is generally reflected in sales for export to Canada of goods of the same class or kind as the goods being appraised made by producers in the country of export.
Amounts included
(3) Without limiting the generality of paragraph (2)(a), the costs, charges, expenses and value referred to in that paragraph include:
(a) the costs, charges and expenses referred to in subparagraph 48(5)(a)(ii);
(b) the value of any of the goods and services referred to in subparagraph 48(5)(a)(iii), determined and apportioned to the goods being appraised as referred to in that subparagraph, whether or not such goods and services have been supplied free of charge or at a reduced cost; and
(c) the costs, charges and expenses incurred by the producer in respect of engineering, development work, art work, design work, plans or sketches undertaken in Canada that were supplied, directly or indirectly, by the purchaser of the goods being appraised for use in connection with the production and sale for export of those goods, apportioned to the goods being appraised as referred to in subparagraph 48(5)(a)(iii).
Definition of
general expenses
(4) For the purposes of this section,
general expenses

Residual Method

Residual basis of appraisal
53 Where the value for duty of goods is not appraised under sections 48 to 52, it shall be appraised on the basis of
(a) a value derived from the method, from among the methods of valuation set out in sections 48 to 52, that, when applied in a flexible manner to the extent necessary to arrive at a value for duty of the goods, conforms closer to the requirements with respect to that method than any other method so applied; and
(b) information available in Canada.

General

Goods exported to Canada through another country
54 For the purposes of sections 45 to 55, where goods are exported to Canada from any country but pass in transit through another country, the goods shall, subject to such terms and conditions as may be prescribed, be deemed to be shipped directly to Canada from the first mentioned country.
R.S., 1985, c. 1 (2nd Supp.), s. 54;
2001, c. 25, s. 38(F).
Value for duty in Canadian currency
55 The value for duty of imported goods shall be computed in Canadian currency in accordance with

regulations made under the
Currency Act
Informing importer of determination of value
56 The importer of any goods, on his written request, shall be informed in writing of the manner in which the value for duty of the goods was determined.

Duties Based on Specific Quantities or Specific Values

Specific quantities or specific values
57 Where duties are imposed on goods according to a specific quantity or a specific value, such duties shall be deemed to apply in the same proportion to any larger or smaller quantity or value, and to any fractional part of such specific quantity or value.

Marking Determination

Marking determination
57.01 (1) Any officer, or any officer within a class of officers, designated by the President for the purposes of this section may, at or before the time goods imported from a NAFTA country are accounted for under subsection 32(1), (3) or (5), in the prescribed manner and subject to the prescribed conditions, make a determination as to whether the goods have been marked in the manner referred to in section 35.01.
Deemed determination
(2) If an officer does not make a determination under subsection (1) in respect of goods imported from a NAFTA country at or before the time the goods are accounted for under subsection 32(1), (3) or (5), a determination as to whether the goods have been marked in the manner referred to in section 35.01 shall be deemed to have been made in accordance with any representations that have been made in respect of the marking of the goods by the person who accounted for the goods.
1993, c. 44, s. 88;
1997, c. 36, s. 165;
2001, c. 25, s. 39;
2005, c. 38, s. 72.

Determination, Re-determination and Further Re-determination of Origin, Tariff Classification and Value for Duty of Imported Goods

Application of sections 58 to 70
57.1 For the purposes of sections 58 to 70,
(a) the origin of imported goods is to be determined in accordance with section 16 of the
Customs Tariff
(b) the tariff classification of imported goods is to be determined in accordance with sections 10 and 11 of the
Customs Tariff
(c) the value for duty of imported goods is to be determined in accordance with sections 47 to 55 of this Act and section 87 of the
Customs Tariff
1988, c. 65, s. 70;
1997, c. 36, s. 166;
2001, c. 25, s. 40.
57.2 Determination by officer
58 (1) Any officer, or any officer within a class of officers, designated by the President for the purposes of this section, may determine the origin, tariff classification and value for duty of imported goods at or before the time they are accounted for under subsection 32(1), (3) or (5).

Deemed determination
(2) If the origin, tariff classification and value for duty of imported goods are not determined under subsection (1), the origin, tariff classification and value for duty of the goods are deemed to be determined, for the purposes of this Act, to be as declared by the person accounting for the goods in the form prescribed under paragraph 32(1)(a). That determination is deemed to be made at the time the goods are accounted for under subsection 32(1), (3) or (5).

Review of determination
(3) A determination made under this section is not subject to be restrained, prohibited, removed, set aside or otherwise dealt with except to the extent and in the manner provided by sections 59 to 61.
R.S., 1985, c. 1 (2nd Supp.), s. 58;
1992, c. 28, s. 11;
1997, c. 36, s. 166;
2005, c. 38, s. 73.

Re-determination or further re-determination
59 (1) An officer, or any officer within a class of officers, designated by the President for the purposes of this section may
(a) in the case of a determination under section 57.01 or 58, re-determine the origin, tariff classification, value for duty or marking determination of any imported goods at any time within
(i) four years after the date of the determination, on the basis of an audit or examination under section 42, a verification under section 42.01 or a verification of origin under section 42.1, or
(ii) four years after the date of the determination, if the Minister considers it advisable to make the re-determination; and
(b) further re-determine the origin, tariff classification or value for duty of imported goods, within four years after the date of the determination or, if the Minister deems it advisable, within such further time as may be prescribed, on the basis of an audit or examination under section 42, a verification under section 42.01 or a verification of origin under section 42.1 that is conducted after the granting of a refund under paragraphs 74(1)(c.1), (c.11), (e), (f) or (g) that is treated by subsection 74(1.1) as a re-determination under paragraph (a) or the making of a correction under section 32.2 that is treated by subsection 32.2(3) as a re-determination under paragraph (a).

Notice requirement
(2) An officer who makes a determination under subsection 57.01(1) or 58(1) or a re-determination or further re-determination under subsection (1) shall without delay give notice of the determination, re-determination or further re-determination, including the rationale on which it is made, to the prescribed persons.

Payment or refund
(3) Every prescribed person who is given notice of a determination, re-determination or further re-determination under subsection (2) shall, in accordance with that decision,
(a) pay any amount owing, or additional amount owing, as the case may be, as duties in respect of the goods or, if a request is made under section 60, pay that amount or give security satisfactory to the Minister in respect of that amount and any interest owing or that may become owing on that amount; or
(b) be given a refund of any duties, or a refund of any duties and interest paid (other than interest that was paid because duties were not paid when required by subsection 32(5) or section 33), in excess of the duties owing in respect of the goods.

Amounts payable immediately
(4) Any amount owing by or to a person under subsection (3) or 66(3) in respect of goods, other than an amount in respect of which security is given, is payable immediately, whether or not a request is made under section 60.

Exception for par. (3)(a)
(5) For the purposes of paragraph (3)(a), the amount owing as duties in respect of goods under subsection (3) as a result of a determination made under subsection 58(1) does not include any amount owing as duties in respect of the goods under section 32 or 33.

Review of re-determination or further re-determination
(6) A re-determination or further re-determination made under this section is not subject to be restrained, prohibited, removed, set aside or otherwise dealt with except to the extent and in the manner provided by subsection 59(1) and sections 60 and 61.
R.S., 1985, c. 1 (2nd Supp.), s. 59;
1997, c. 36, s. 166;
2001, c. 25, s. 41;
2005, c. 38, s. 74.

Re-determination and Further Re-determination by President

Request for re-determination or further re-determination
60 (1) A person to whom notice is given under subsection 59(2) in respect of goods may, within ninety days after the notice is given, request a re-determination or further re-determination of origin, tariff classification, value for duty or marking. The request may be made only after all amounts owing as duties and interest in respect of the goods are paid or security satisfactory to the Minister is given in respect of the total amount owing.
Request for review
(2) A person may request a review of an advance ruling made under section 43.1 within ninety days after it is given to the person.
How request to be made
(3) A request under this section must be made to the President in the prescribed form and manner, with the prescribed information.
President's duty on receipt of request
(4) On receipt of a request under this section, the President shall, without delay,
(a) re-determine or further re-determine the origin, tariff classification or value for duty;
(b) affirm, revise or reverse the advance ruling; or
(c) re-determine or further re-determine the marking determination.
Notice requirement
(5) The President shall without delay give notice of a decision made under subsection (4), including the rationale on which the decision is made, to the person who made the request.
R.S., 1985, c. 1 (2nd Supp.), s. 60;
1992, c. 28, s. 12;
1997, c. 36, s. 166;
1999, c. 17, s. 127;
2001, c. 25, s. 42;
2005, c. 38, s. 85.
Extension of time to make a request
60.1 (1) If no request is made under section 60 within the time set out in that section, a person may make an application to the President for an extension of the time within which the request may be made, and the President may extend the time for making the request.
Reasons
(2) The application must set out the reasons why the request was not made on time.
How application made
(3) The application must be made to the President in the prescribed manner and form and contain the prescribed information.
Duties of President
(4) On receipt of an application, the President must, without delay, consider it and notify the person making the application, in writing, of the President's decision.
Date of request
(5) If the President grants the application, the request is valid as of the date of the President's decision.

Conditions for granting application
(6) No application may be granted unless
(a) the application is made within one year after the expiry of the time set out in section 60; and
(b) the person making the application demonstrates that
(i) within the time set out in section 60, the person was unable to act or to give a mandate to act in the person's name or the person had a
(ii) it would be just and equitable to grant the application, and
(iii) the application was made as soon as circumstances permitted.
2001, c. 25, s. 43;
2005, c. 38, s. 85.
Extension of time by Canadian International Trade Tribunal
60.2 (1) A person who has made an application under section 60.1 may apply to the Canadian International Trade Tribunal to have the application granted after either
(a) the President has refused the application; or
(b) ninety days have elapsed after the application was made and the President has not notified the person of the President's decision.
If paragraph (a) applies, the application under this subsection must be made within ninety days after the application is refused.
How application made
(2) The application must be made by filing with the President and the Canadian International Trade Tribunal a copy of the application referred to in section 60.1 and, if notice has been given under subsection 60.1(4), a copy of the notice.
Powers of Canadian International Trade Tribunal
(3) The Canadian International Trade Tribunal may dispose of an application by dismissing or granting it and, in granting an application, it may impose any terms that it considers just or order that the request be deemed to be a valid request as of the date of the order.
When application to be granted
(4) No application may be granted under this section unless
(a) the application under subsection 60.1(1) was made within one year after the expiry of the time set out in section 60; and
(b) the person making the application demonstrates that
(i) within the time set out in section 60, the person was unable to act or to give a mandate to act in the person's name or the person had a
(ii) it would be just and equitable to grant the application, and
(iii) the application was made as soon as circumstances permitted.
2001, c. 25, s. 43;
2005, c. 38, s. 85;
2014, c. 20, s. 446.
What President may do
61 (1) The President may
(a) re-determine or further re-determine the origin, tariff classification or value for duty of imported goods
(i) at any time after a re-determination or further re-determination is made under paragraph 60(4)(a), but before an appeal is heard under section 67, on the recommendation of the Attorney General of Canada, if the re-determination or further re-determination would reduce duties payable on the goods,
(ii) at any time, if the person who accounted for the goods under subsection 32(1), (3) or (5) fails to comply with any provision of this Act or the regulations or commits an offence under this Act in respect of the goods, and
(iii) at any time, if the re-determination or further re-determination would give effect to a decision of the Canadian International Trade Tribunal, the Federal Court of Appeal or the Supreme Court of Canada made in respect of the goods;

(b) re-determine or further re-determine the marking determination of imported goods
(i) within four years after the date the determination was made under section 57.01, if the Minister considers it advisable to make the re-determination,
(ii) at any time, if the person who is given notice of a marking determination under section 57.01 or of a re-determination under paragraph 59(1)(a) fails to comply with any provision of this Act or the regulations or commits an offence under this Act in respect of the goods,
(iii) at any time, if the re-determination or further re-determination would give effect to a decision made in respect of the goods by the Canadian International Trade Tribunal, the Federal Court of Appeal or the Supreme Court of Canada, and
(iv) at any time after a re-determination is made under paragraph 60(4)(c), but before an appeal is heard under section 67, on the recommendation of the Attorney General of Canada; and
(c) re-determine or further re-determine the origin, tariff classification or value for duty of imported goods (in this paragraph referred to as the "subsequent goods"), at any time, if the re-determination or further re-determination would give effect, in respect of the subsequent goods, to a decision of the Canadian International Trade Tribunal, the Federal Court of Appeal or the Supreme Court of Canada, or of the President under subparagraph (a)(i),
(i) that relates to the origin or tariff classification of other like goods imported by the same importer or owner on or before the date of importation of the subsequent goods, or
(ii) that relates to the manner of determining the value for duty of other goods previously imported by the same importer or owner on or before the date of importation of the subsequent goods.

Notice requirement
(2) If the President makes a re-determination or further re-determination under this section, the President shall without delay give notice of that decision, including the rationale on which the decision is made, to the prescribed persons.
R.S., 1985, c. 1 (2nd Supp.), s. 61;
1992, c. 28, s. 13;
1993, c. 44, s. 92;
1997, c. 36, s. 166;
1999, c. 17, s. 127;
2001, c. 25, s. 44;
2005, c. 38, s. 85.

No review
62 A re-determination or further re-determination under section 60 or 61 is not subject to be restrained, prohibited, removed, set aside or otherwise dealt with except to the extent and in the manner provided by section 67.
R.S., 1985, c. 1 (2nd Supp.), s. 62;
1992, c. 28, s. 14;
1993, c. 44, s. 93;
1997, c. 36, s. 166.

63 and 64 Payment or refund
65 (1) If a re-determination or further re-determination is made under paragraph 60(4)(a) or 61(1)(a) or (c) in respect of goods, such persons who are given notice of the decision as may be prescribed shall, in accordance with the decision,
(a) pay any additional amount owing as duties in respect of the goods or, where an appeal is taken under section 67, give security satisfactory to the Minister in respect of that amount and any interest owing or that may become owing on that amount; or
(b) be given a refund of any duties and interest paid (other than interest that was paid by reason of duties not being paid in accordance with subsection 32(5) or section 33) in excess of the duties and interest owing in respect of the goods.

Amount owing or refund payable immediately
(2) Any amount owing by or to a person under subsection (1) or 66(3) of this Act or as a result of a determination or re-determination under the

Special Import Measures Act
(3) R.S., 1985, c. 1 (2nd Supp.), s. 65;
1992, c. 28, s. 16;
1993, c. 44, s. 96(E);
1997, c. 36, s. 167;
2001, c. 25, s. 45.

Refund to person other than payer
65.1 (1) If a person (in this subsection referred to as the "applicant") to whom notice of a decision under subsection 59(1) or paragraph 60(4)(a) or 61(1)(a) or (c) was given would be entitled under paragraph 59(3)(b) or 65(1)(b) to a refund of an amount if the applicant had been the person who paid the amount, the amount may be paid to the applicant and any amount so paid to the applicant is deemed to have been refunded to the applicant under that paragraph.

Effect of refund
(2) If an amount in respect of goods has been refunded to a person under paragraph 59(3)(b) or 65(1)(b), no other person is entitled to a refund of an amount in respect of the goods under either of those paragraphs.

Exception — marking determinations
(3) This section does not apply to a marking determination.
1992, c. 28, s. 17;
1997, c. 36, s. 168;
2001, c. 25, s. 46.

Interest on payments
66 (1) If the amount paid by a person on account of duties expected to be owing under paragraph 59(3)(a) or 65(1)(a) of this Act or under the
Special Import Measures Act

Interest where security given
(2) If, as a result of a determination, re-determination or further re-determination made in respect of goods, a person is required under paragraph 59(3)(a) or 65(1)(a) to pay an amount owing as duties in respect of the goods and the person gives security under that paragraph pending a subsequent re-determination or further re-determination in respect of the goods, the interest payable under subsection 33.4(1) on any amount owing as a result of the subsequent re-determination or further re-determination is to be computed at the prescribed rate for the period beginning on the first day after the day the security was given and ending on the day the subsequent re-determination or further re-determination is made.

Interest on refunds
(3) A person who is given a refund under paragraph 59(3)(b) or 65(1)(b) of this Act or under the
Special Import Measures Act
R.S., 1985, c. 1 (2nd Supp.), s. 66;
1992, c. 28, s. 18;
1997, c. 36, s. 168;
2001, c. 25, s. 47.

Appeals and References

Appeal to the Canadian International Trade Tribunal
67 (1) A person aggrieved by a decision of the President made under section 60 or 61 may appeal from the decision to the Canadian International Trade Tribunal by filing a notice of appeal in writing with the President and the Canadian International Trade Tribunal within ninety days after the time notice of the decision was given.

Publication of notice of appeal
(2) Before making a decision under this section, the Canadian International Trade Tribunal shall provide for a hearing and shall publish a notice thereof in the

Canada Gazette

Judicial review

(3) On an appeal under subsection (1), the Canadian International Trade Tribunal may make such order, finding or declaration as the nature of the matter may require, and an order, finding or declaration made under this section is not subject to review or to be restrained, prohibited, removed, set aside or otherwise dealt with except to the extent and in the manner provided by section 68.

R.S., 1985, c. 1 (2nd Supp.), s. 67, c. 47 (4th Supp.), s. 52;
1997, c. 36, s. 169;
1999, c. 17, s. 127;
2001, c. 25, s. 48(F);
2005, c. 38, s. 85;
2014, c. 20, s. 446.

Extension of time to appeal

67.1 (1) If no notice of appeal has been filed within the time set out in section 67, a person may make an application to the Canadian International Trade Tribunal for an order extending the time within which a notice of appeal may be filed, and the Tribunal may make an order extending the time for appealing and may impose any terms that it considers just.

Reasons

(2) The application must set out the reasons why the notice of appeal was not filed on time.

How application made

(3) The application must be made by filing with the President and the Canadian International Trade Tribunal the application accompanied by the notice of appeal.

Conditions for granting application

(4) No order may be made under this section unless

(a) the application is made within one year after the expiry of the time set out in section 67; and

(b) the person making the application demonstrates that

(i) within the time set out in section 67 for appealing, the person was unable to act or to give a mandate to act in the person's name or the person had a

(ii) it would be just and equitable to grant the application,

(iii) the application was made as soon as circumstances permitted, and

(iv) there are reasonable grounds for the appeal.

2001, c. 25, s. 49;
2005, c. 38, s. 85;
2014, c. 20, s. 446.

Appeal to Federal Court

68 (1) Any of the parties to an appeal under section 67, namely,

(a) the person who appealed,

(b) the President, or

(c) any person who entered an appearance in accordance with subsection 67(2),

may, within ninety days after the date a decision is made under section 67, appeal therefrom to the Federal Court of Appeal on any question of law.

Disposition of appeal

(2) The Federal Court of Appeal may dispose of an appeal by making such order or finding as the nature of the matter may require or by referring the matter back to the Canadian International Trade Tribunal for re-hearing.

R.S., 1985, c. 1 (2nd Supp.), s. 68, c. 47 (4th Supp.), s. 52;
1995, c. 41, s. 20;
1999, c. 17, s. 127;
2005, c. 38, s. 85.

Refund pending appeal

69 (1) Where an appeal is taken under section 67 or 68 in respect of goods and the person who appeals has paid any amount as duties and interest in respect of the goods, the person shall, on giving

security satisfactory to the Minister in respect of the unpaid portion of the duties and interest owing in respect of the goods and the whole or any portion of the amount paid as duties and interest (other than interest that was paid by reason of duties not being paid in accordance with subsection 32(5) or section 33) in respect of the goods, be given a refund of the whole or any portion of the amount paid in respect of which security is given.

Interest

(2) Where a refund is given under subsection (1), the person who is given the refund shall,

(a) if a re-determination or further re-determination is made by the President under subparagraph 61(1)(a)(iii) and a portion of the amount refunded as a result of that decision is owing as duties and interest, pay interest at the prescribed rate for the period beginning on the first day after the day the refund is given and ending on the day the amount of the refund found to be owing as duties and interest has been paid in full, calculated on the outstanding balance of that amount of the refund, except that if the amount of the refund found to be owing is paid within thirty days after the day that decision is made, interest shall not be payable on that amount from that day to the day the amount is paid; or

(b) if a re-determination or further re-determination is made by the President under subparagraph 61(1)(a)(iii) and a portion of the amount refunded as a result of that decision is not owing as duties and interest, be given interest at the prescribed rate for the period beginning on the day after the amount refunded was originally paid by that person and ending on the day it was refunded, calculated on the amount of the refund found not to be owing.

R.S., 1985, c. 1 (2nd Supp.), s. 69, c. 1 (4th Supp.), s. 45(F);

1992, c. 28, s. 19;

1997, c. 36, s. 170;

1999, c. 17, s. 127;

2001, c. 25, s. 50(F);

2005, c. 38, s. 85.

References to Canadian International Trade Tribunal

70 (1) The President may refer to the Canadian International Trade Tribunal for its opinion any questions relating to the origin, tariff classification or value for duty of any goods or class of goods.

Idem

(2) Sections 67 and 68 apply in respect of a reference made pursuant to this section as if the reference were an appeal taken pursuant to section 67.

R.S., 1985, c. 1 (2nd Supp.), s. 70, c. 47 (4th Supp.), s. 52;

1997, c. 36, s. 171;

1999, c. 17, s. 127;

2005, c. 38, s. 85.

Special Provisions

Special provisions

71 (1) If the release of goods is refused because the goods have been determined to be prohibited goods classified under tariff item No. 9899.00.00 of the List of Tariff Provisions set out in the schedule to the

Customs Tariff

(a) subparagraph 61(1)(a)(iii) and paragraph 61(1)(c) are deemed to include a reference to the court; and

(b) in sections 67 and 68, the expression "court" is deemed to be substituted for the expression "Canadian International Trade Tribunal".

Definitions

(2) In this section,

clerk of the court

court

(a) in the Province of Ontario, the Superior Court of Justice,
(b) in the Province of Quebec, the Superior Court,
(c) in the Provinces of Nova Scotia, British Columbia and Prince Edward Island, in Yukon and in the Northwest Territories, the Supreme Court,
(d) in the Provinces of New Brunswick, Manitoba, Saskatchewan and Alberta, the Court of Queen's Bench,
(e) (f) in the Province of Newfoundland and Labrador, the Trial Division of the Supreme Court, and
(g) in Nunavut, the Nunavut Court of Justice.
R.S., 1985, c. 1 (2nd Supp.), s. 71, c. 41 (3rd Supp.), s. 120, c. 47 (4th Supp.), s. 52;
1990, c. 16, s. 8, c. 17, s. 16;
1992, c. 1, s. 61, c. 51, s. 44;
1997, c. 36, s. 172;
1998, c. 30, ss. 12, 14;
1999, c. 3, s. 59;
2002, c. 7, s. 152;
2014, c. 20, s. 445;
2015, c. 3, s. 61.

Limitation relating to security
72 No security may be given under paragraph 59(3)(a) or 65(1)(a) or subsection 69(1) in respect of any amount owing as surtaxes levied under section 53, 55, 60, 63, 68 or 78 of the
Customs Tariff
R.S., 1985, c. 1 (2nd Supp.), s. 72, c. 41 (3rd Supp.), s. 121;
1988, c. 65, s. 71;
1993, c. 44, s. 97;
1996, c. 33, s. 35;
1997, c. 14, s. 42, c. 36, s. 173.

Limitation — heading No. 98.26 of List of Tariff Provisions
72.1 Notwithstanding subsection 59(1) and sections 60 and 61, no re-determination or further re-determination of the tariff classification of imported goods classified under heading No. 98.26 of the List of Tariff Provisions set out in the schedule to the
Customs Tariff
(a) change the classification of the goods to another tariff item under that heading; or
(b) change the classification of all those goods accounted for under the same accounting document to tariff items in Chapters 1 to 97 of that List.
1990, c. 36, s. 1;
1997, c. 36, s. 173.
72.2

PART IV

PART IV
Abatements and Refunds

Abatement
73 Subject to section 75 and any regulations made under section 81, the Minister may grant an abatement of the whole or part of the duties on imported goods where the goods have suffered
(a) damage, deterioration or destruction at any time from the time of shipment to Canada to the time of release; or
(b) a loss in volume or weight arising from natural causes while in a bonded warehouse.

Refund
74 (1) Subject to this section, section 75 and any regulations made under section 81, a person who paid duties on any imported goods may, in accordance with subsection (3), apply for a refund of all or part of those duties, and the Minister may grant to that person a refund of all or part of those

duties, if

(a) they have suffered damage, deterioration or destruction at any time from the time of shipment to Canada to the time of release;
(b) the quantity released is less than the quantity in respect of which duties were paid;
(c) they are of a quality inferior to that in respect of which duties were paid;
(c.1) the goods were exported from a NAFTA country or from Chile but no claim for preferential tariff treatment under NAFTA or no claim for preferential tariff treatment under CCFTA, as the case may be, was made in respect of those goods at the time they were accounted for under subsection 32(1), (3) or (5);
(c.11) the goods were imported from Israel or another CIFTA beneficiary or from a country or territory set out in column 1 of Part 4 of the schedule but no claim for preferential tariff treatment under CIFTA or an agreement set out in column 2, as the case may be, was made in respect of those goods at the time they were accounted for under subsection 32(1), (3) or (5);
(c.2) (d) the calculation of duties owing was based on a clerical, typographical or similar error;
(e) the duties were paid or overpaid as a result of an error in the determination under subsection 58(2) of origin (other than in the circumstances described in paragraph (c.1) or (c.11)), tariff classification or value for duty in respect of the goods and the determination has not been the subject of a decision under any of sections 59 to 61;
(f) the goods, or other goods into which they have been incorporated, are sold or otherwise disposed of to a person, or are used, in compliance with a condition imposed under a tariff item in the List of Tariff Provisions set out in the schedule to the
Customs Tariff
(g) the duties were overpaid or paid in error for any reason that may be prescribed.

Refund treated as re-determination

(1.1) The granting of a refund under paragraph (1)(c.1), (c.11), (e) or (f) or, if the refund is based on tariff classification, value for duty or origin, under paragraph (1)(g) is to be treated for the purposes of this Act, other than section 66, as if it were a re-determination made under paragraph 59(1)(a).

Duties

(1.2) The duties that may be refunded under paragraph (1)(f) do not include duties or taxes levied under the
Excise Act, 2001
Excise Tax Act
Special Import Measures Act

Claims for refund

(2) No refund shall be granted under any of paragraphs (1)(a) to (c) and (d) in respect of a claim unless written notice of the claim and the reason for it is given to an officer within the prescribed time.

Idem

(3) No refund shall be granted under subsection (1) in respect of a claim unless
(a) the person making the claim affords an officer reasonable opportunity to examine the goods in respect of which the claim is made or otherwise verify the reason for the claim; and
(b) an application for the refund, including such evidence in support of the application as may be prescribed, is made to an officer in the prescribed manner and in the prescribed form containing the prescribed information within
(i) in the case of an application for a refund under paragraph (1)(a), (b), (c), (c.11), (d), (e), (f) or (g), four years after the goods were accounted for under subsection 32(1), (3) or (5), and
(ii) in the case of an application for a refund under paragraph (1)(c.1), one year after the goods were accounted for under subsection 32(1), (3) or (5) or such longer period as may be prescribed.

Effect of denial of refund

(4) A denial of an application for a refund of duties paid on goods is to be treated for the purposes of this Act as if it were a re-determination under paragraph 59(1)(a) if
(a) the application is for a refund under paragraph (1)(c.1) or (c.11) and the application is denied

because at the time the goods were accounted for under subsection 32(1), (3) or (5), they were not eligible for preferential tariff treatment under a free trade agreement; or

(b) the application is for a refund under paragraph (1)(e), (f) or (g) and the application is denied because the origin, tariff classification or value for duty of the goods as claimed in the application is incorrect.

(4.1) Effect of denial of refund
(5) For greater certainty, a denial of an application for a refund under paragraph (1)(c.1), (c.11), (e), (f) or (g) on the basis that complete or accurate documentation has not been provided, or on any ground other than the ground specified in subsection (4), is not to be treated for the purposes of this Act as if it were a re-determination under this Act of origin, tariff classification or value for duty.

Refund without application
(6) The Minister, within four years after goods are accounted for under subsection 32(1), (3) or (5), may refund all or part of duties paid on imported goods without application by the person who paid them if it is determined that the duties were overpaid or paid in error in any of the circumstances set out in

(a) paragraphs (1)(a) to (c) or (d); or
(b) paragraph (1)(g), only to the extent that the refund is not based on tariff classification, value for duty or origin of the goods.

Duties that may not be refunded
(7) The duties that may be refunded under subsection (6) do not include duties or taxes levied under the

Excise Act
Excise Tax Act
Special Import Measures Act
Customs Tariff

Application of refund
(8) A person of a prescribed class may apply, within four years after goods are accounted for under subsection 32(1), (3) or (5), in prescribed circumstances and under prescribed conditions, the amount of any refund to which they are entitled under this section to the payment of any amount for which they are liable or may become liable under this Act.

R.S., 1985, c. 1 (2nd Supp.), s. 74;
1988, c. 65, s. 72;
1993, c. 44, s. 98;
1996, c. 33, s. 36;
1997, c. 14, s. 43, c. 36, s. 175;
1999, c. 31, s. 71(F);
2001, c. 25, s. 51, c. 28, s. 29;
2002, c. 22, s. 337;
2009, c. 6, s. 27, c. 16, ss. 34, 56;
2010, c. 4, s. 28;
2012, c. 18, s. 29.

74.1 Amount of abatement or refund
75 (1) Subject to sections 78 and 79, the amount of any abatement or refund granted under section 73 or 74 shall be determined in accordance with such regulations as the Governor in Council may make prescribing the methods of determining the amount and the classes of cases to which such determinations apply.

Alternative rule for case of deficiency
(2) Where the quantity of imported goods released is less than the quantity in respect of which duties were paid and no refund of duties has been granted in respect of the deficient quantity, an officer may, in such circumstances as may be prescribed and at the request of the person by whom the duties were paid, apply any duties paid in respect of the deficient quantity of the goods to any duties that become due on the deficient quantity if any portion thereof is subsequently imported by the same

importer or owner.
Refunds for defective goods
76 (1) Subject to any regulations made under section 81, the Minister may, in such circumstances as may be prescribed, grant to any person by whom duties were paid on imported goods that are defective, are of a quality inferior to that in respect of which duties were paid or are not the goods ordered, a refund of the whole or part of the duties paid thereon if the goods have, subsequently to the importation, been disposed of in a manner acceptable to the Minister at no expense to Her Majesty in right of Canada or exported.
Subsections 74(2) and (3) and 75(1) apply
(2) Subsections 74(2) and (3) and 75(1) apply, with such modifications as the circumstances require, in respect of refunds under this section.
R.S., 1985, c. 1 (2nd Supp.), s. 76;
2001, c. 25, s. 52(F).
77 Merchantable scrap, waste or by-products
78 In such circumstances as may be prescribed, where merchantable scrap, waste or by-products result from the destruction or disposal of goods or from the incorporation of goods into other goods, the amount of any abatement or refund that is granted in respect of such goods under this Act by virtue of the destruction, disposal or incorporation into other goods shall be reduced by an amount determined in the prescribed manner.
R.S., 1985, c. 1 (2nd Supp.), s. 78;
1992, c. 1, s. 144(F).
Sum in lieu of refund or abatement
79 Where circumstances exist that render it difficult to determine the exact amount of any abatement or refund that should be granted in respect of goods under this Act, the Minister may, with the consent of the person claiming the abatement or refund, grant to that person, in lieu thereof, a specific sum, the amount of which shall be determined by the Minister.
Certain duties not included
79.1 For the purposes of sections 78 and 79, an abatement or refund does not include a rebate or refund of any amount paid in respect of tax levied under Part IX of the
Excise Tax Act
1990, c. 45, s. 20.
Interest on refunds
80 Any person who is granted a refund of duties under section 74, 76 or 79 shall be granted, in addition to the refund, interest on the refund at the prescribed rate for the period beginning on the ninety-first day after the day an application for the refund is received in accordance with paragraph 74(3)(b) and ending on the day the refund is granted.
R.S., 1985, c. 1 (2nd Supp.), s. 80;
1992, c. 28, s. 20;
1997, c. 36, s. 178;
2001, c. 25, s. 53.
Interest on past refunds
80.1 Notwithstanding subsection 80(1), any person who, under paragraph 74(1)(g), is granted a refund of duties on imported goods on which the rate of customs duty is reduced by a retroactive order or regulation of the Governor in Council made under the
Customs Tariff
1990, c. 36, s. 3;
1992, c. 28, s. 21;
1997, c. 36, s. 179.
Excess to be repaid
80.2 (1) Subject to subsection (2), if an abatement or refund is granted to a person under sections 73 to 76 and the person is not entitled to all or part of it, the person is liable to repay the amount to which they are not entitled to Her Majesty in right of Canada, on the day it is received by the person,

together with any interest that was granted to the person under section 80 or 80.1 on that amount.
Excess to be repaid — paragraph 74(1)(f)
(2) If an abatement or refund is granted to a person under paragraph 74(1)(f) and the goods are sold or otherwise disposed of or are subsequently used in a manner that fails to comply with a condition imposed under a tariff item in the List of Tariff Provisions set out in the schedule to the Customs Tariff
(a) report the failure to an officer at a customs office; and
(b) pay to Her Majesty in right of Canada any amount to which they are not entitled, together with any interest that was granted to the person under section 80 or 80.1 on that amount.
1997, c. 36, s. 180;
2001, c. 25, s. 54.
Regulations
81 The Governor in Council may make regulations prescribing the circumstances in which abatements or refunds shall not be granted under this Act in respect of prescribed classes of goods.
82 to 87 88 to 91 92 93 and 94
PART V

PART V
Exportation

Report
95 (1) Subject to paragraph (2)(a), all goods that are exported shall be reported at such time and place and in such manner as may be prescribed.
Regulations
(2) The Governor in Council may prescribe
(a) the classes of goods that are exempted from the requirements of subsection (1) and the circumstances in which any of those classes of goods are not so exempted; and
(b) the classes of persons who are required to report goods under subsection (1) and the circumstances in which they are so required.
Obligation to answer questions and present goods
(3) Every person reporting goods under subsection (1) shall
(a) answer truthfully any question asked by an officer with respect to the goods; and
(b) where an officer so requests, present the goods to the officer, remove any covering from the goods, unload any conveyance or open any part thereof, or open or unpack any package or container that the officer wishes to examine.
Written report
(4) If goods are required to be reported in writing, they shall be reported in the prescribed form containing the prescribed information or in such form containing such information as is satisfactory to the Minister.
R.S., 1985, c. 1 (2nd Supp.), s. 95;
2001, c. 25, s. 55.
Statistics
95.1 (1) Subject to this section, every person who reports goods under subsection 95(1) shall, at the time of reporting, furnish an officer at a customs office with the statistical code for the goods determined by reference to the Coding System established pursuant to section 22.1 of the Statistics Act
Prescribed form
(2) The statistical code referred to in subsection (1) shall be furnished in the prescribed manner and in the prescribed form containing the prescribed information.
Regulations
(3) The Governor in Council may make regulations exempting persons or goods, or classes thereof, from the requirements of subsection (1) subject to such conditions, if any, as are specified in the

regulations.
1988, c. 65, s. 77.
Failure to export
96 Where goods are reported under section 95 and not duly exported, the person who reported them shall forthwith report the failure to export them to an officer at a customs office.
Security
97 In such circumstances as may be prescribed, goods that are transported within Canada after they have been reported under section 95 shall be transported subject to such conditions and subject to such bonds or other security as may be prescribed.
97.01 Certificate of Origin of goods exported to a free trade partner
97.1 (1) Every exporter of goods to a free trade partner for which preferential tariff treatment under a free trade agreement will be claimed in accordance with the laws of that free trade partner shall certify in writing in the prescribed form and containing the prescribed information that goods exported or to be exported from Canada to that free trade partner meet the rules of origin set out in, or contemplated by, the applicable free trade agreement and, if the exporter is not the producer of the goods, the certificate shall be completed and signed by the exporter on the basis of the prescribed criteria.
Provision of copy of Certificate of Origin
(2) Every exporter or producer of goods who, for the purpose of enabling any person to comply with the applicable laws relating to customs of a free trade partner, completes and signs a certificate in accordance with subsection (1) shall, at the request of an officer, provide the officer with a copy of the certificate.
Notification of correct information
(3) A person who has completed and signed a certificate in accordance with subsection (1) and who has reason to believe that it contains incorrect information shall immediately notify all persons to whom the certificate was given of the correct information.
1988, c. 65, s. 78;
1997, c. 14, s. 44;
2001, c. 25, s. 56(F).
97.11 Exporters' or producers' records
97.2 (1) Every person who exports goods or causes them to be exported for sale or for any industrial, occupational, commercial, institutional or other like use or any other use that may be prescribed, and every other person who has completed and signed a certificate in accordance with subsection 97.1(1), shall keep at the person's place of business in Canada or at any other place that may be designated by the Minister any records in respect of those goods in the manner and for the period that may be prescribed and shall, if an officer requests, make them available to the officer, within the time specified by the officer, and answer any questions asked by the officer in respect of the records.
Idem
(2) Subsection 40(2) and sections 42 and 43 apply, with such modifications as the circumstances require, to a person required to keep records pursuant to subsection (1).
1988, c. 65, s. 78;
1993, c. 44, s. 104;
1996, c. 33, s. 38;
1997, c. 14, s. 45;
2001, c. 25, s. 57.
Verification of origin — certain agreements
97.201 (1) The customs administration of any state or beneficiary referred to in subsection 42.1(1.1) to which goods were exported may request in writing that the Agency conduct a verification and provide, as the case may be
(a) an opinion as to whether those goods are originating within the meaning of Annex C of CEFTA;
(b) a written report as to whether the goods are originating within the meaning of Chapter 3 of CUFTA; or

(c) a written report as to whether the goods are originating within the meaning of the Protocol on Rules of Origin and Origin Procedures of CETA.

Methods of verification

(2) Any officer, or any officer within a class of officers, designated by the President for the purposes of this section, or any person, or any person within a class of persons, designated by the President to act on behalf of such an officer, may, subject to any prescribed conditions, conduct a verification of origin of goods referred to in subsection (1)

(a) by entering any prescribed premises or place at any reasonable time; or

(b) in any other prescribed manner.

Statement of origin — certain agreements

(3) On completion of a verification of origin requested under subsection (1), an officer or other person designated under subsection (2) shall

(a) provide, in the prescribed manner, the customs administration of the state or beneficiary with the opinion or written report requested and any relevant supporting documents that may be requested by that customs administration; and

(b) determine whether the goods are originating within the meaning of the applicable provision referred to in subsection (1).

Notice requirement

(4) The President shall without delay give notice of a decision made under paragraph (3)(b), including the rationale on which the decision is made, to the exporter or producer of the goods, as the case may be, subject to the verification of origin.

Determination treated as re-determination

(5) A determination made under paragraph (3)(b) is to be treated for the purposes of this Act as if it were a re-determination under paragraph 59(1)(a).

2009, c. 6, s. 28;

2017, c. 6, s. 84, c. 8, ss. 22, 43.

PART V.1

PART V.1
Collections

Interpretation

Definitions

97.21 The definitions in this section apply in this Part.

Commissioner

Canada Revenue Agency Act

debtor

judge

Minister

receiver

(a) under the authority of a debenture, bond or other debt security, a court order or an Act of Parliament or of the legislature of a province, is empowered to operate or manage a business or a property of another person;

(b) is appointed by a trustee under a trust deed in respect of a debt security to exercise the authority of the trustee to manage or operate a business or a property of the debtor under the debt security;

(c) is appointed by a bank to act as agent of the bank in the exercise of the authority of the bank under subsection 426(3) of the

Bank Act

(d) is appointed as a liquidator to liquidate the assets of a corporation or to wind up the affairs of a corporation; or

(e) is appointed as a committee, guardian or curator with authority to manage and care for the affairs and assets of an individual who is incapable of managing those affairs and assets.
It includes a person who is appointed to exercise the authority of a creditor under a debenture, bond or other debt security to operate or manage a business or a property of another person. However, if a person is so appointed it does not include that creditor.
2001, c. 25, s. 58;
2005, c. 38, s. 75.

Ancillary Powers

Ancillary powers
97.211 (1) The Minister may, for the purposes of administering or enforcing this Part, exercise any of the following powers that are necessary for the collection of debts due to Her Majesty under this Part:
(a) the powers provided for in paragraphs (a) and (b) of the definition
prescribed
(b) any other powers that are conferred under any provision of this Act that is specified by the Governor in Council on the recommendation of the Minister and the Minister of Public Safety and Emergency Preparedness.
Publication
(2) An order made for the purpose of subsection (1) must be published in Part II of the Canada Gazette
2005, c. 38, ss. 76, 145.

General

Debts to Her Majesty
97.22 (1) Subject to subsections (2) and (3), any duties, fee, charge or other amount owing or payable under this Act is a debt due to Her Majesty in right of Canada from and after the time such amount should have been paid, and any person from whom the amount is owing shall, after a notice of arrears is sent by mail addressed to the person at their latest known address or delivered to that address, pay the amount owing as indicated in the notice or appeal the notice under section 97.23.
Penalty or ascertained forfeiture
(2) Any amount of money demanded as a penalty in a notice of assessment served under section 109.3 and any interest payable under section 109.5 or any amount of money demanded in a notice under section 124 and any interest payable under subsection 124(6), from and after the time of service, is a debt due to Her Majesty in right of Canada from the person on whom the notice is served and the person shall pay that amount or, within ninety days after the time of service, request a decision of the Minister of Public Safety and Emergency Preparedness under section 131.
Amounts demanded
(3) Any amount of money demanded under paragraph 133(1)(c) or (1.1)(b) and any interest payable under subsection 133(7), from and after the time notice is served under subsection 131(2), is a debt due to Her Majesty in right of Canada from the person who requested the decision and the person shall pay the amount so demanded or, if the person appeals the decision of the Minister of Public Safety and Emergency Preparedness under section 135, give security satisfactory to that Minister.
Court costs
(4) If an amount is payable by a person to Her Majesty in right of Canada because of an order, judgment or award of a court in respect of the costs of litigation relating to a matter to which this Act applies, sections 97.24, 97.26, 97.28 and 97.3 to 97.33 apply to the amount as if the amount were a debt owing by the person to Her Majesty on account of duties payable by the person under this Act.
Court
(5) Any amount payable under this Act is recoverable in the Federal Court or any other court of

competent jurisdiction or in any other manner provided under this Part.
Interest on judgments
(6) If a judgment is obtained for any amount payable under this Act, including a certificate registered under section 97.24, the provisions of this Act under which interest is payable for failure to pay the amount apply, with any modifications that the circumstances require, to a failure to pay the judgment debt, and the interest is recoverable in the same manner as the judgment debt.
2001, c. 25, s. 58;
2005, c. 38, ss. 77, 84, 145.
Appeal
97.23 A person to whom a notice is sent or delivered under subsection 97.22(1) may, within thirty days after that notice is sent, appeal the notice by way of an action in the Federal Court in which the person is the plaintiff and the Minister of Public Safety and Emergency Preparedness is the defendant if
(a) no appeal is or was available to that person under section 67 or 68 in respect of the same matter; and
(b) the notice is not in respect of an amount assessed under section 97.44.
2001, c. 25, s. 58;
2005, c. 38, ss. 84, 145.

Certificates, Liens and Set-off

Certificate
97.24 (1) Any debt, or any part of a debt, due to Her Majesty in right of Canada under this Act may be certified by the Minister as an amount payable by the debtor.
Registration in court
(2) On production to the Federal Court, the certificate must be registered in the Court. When it is registered, it has the same force and effect, and all proceedings may be taken, as if the certificate were a judgment obtained in the Court for a debt of the amount specified in the certificate and interest on the amount as provided under this Act. For the purposes of any such proceedings, the certificate is a judgment of the Court against the debtor and enforceable as such.
Costs
(3) All reasonable costs and charges for the registration of the certificate or in respect of any proceedings taken to collect the amount certified are recoverable in the same way as if they had been certified in the certificate registered under this section.
Protected interest in property
(4) A memorial may be recorded for the purpose of creating a protected interest in property in a province or an interest in such property held by the debtor in the same manner as a document evidencing the following may be recorded in accordance with the law of the province:
(a) a judgment of the superior court of the province against a person for a debt owing by the person; and
(b) an amount payable by a person in the province in respect of a debt owing to Her Majesty in right of the province.
Creation of protected interest
(5) The effect of recording a memorial is, in the same manner and to the same extent as if the memorial were a document evidencing a judgment or an amount referred to in subsection (4), to create a protected interest in the property of the debtor in the province, or in any interest in that property, held by the debtor or to otherwise bind that property or interest in the property. The protected interest created is subordinate to any protected interest in respect of which all steps necessary to make it effective against other creditors were taken before the time the memorial was recorded.
Proceedings in respect of memorial
(6) If a memorial is recorded in a province, proceedings may be taken, in the same manner and to the

same extent as if the memorial were a document evidencing a judgment or an amount referred to in subsection (4), in the province in respect of the memorial, including proceedings
(a) to enforce payment of the amount evidenced by the memorial, interest on the amount and all costs and charges paid or incurred in respect of the recording of the memorial and proceedings taken to collect the amount;
(b) to renew or otherwise prolong the effectiveness of the recording of the memorial;
(c) to cancel or withdraw the memorial wholly or in respect of any of the property or interests affected by the memorial; or
(d) to postpone the effectiveness of the recording of the memorial in favour of any protected interest that has been or is intended to be recorded in respect of any property or interest affected by the memorial.

Federal Court may make order, etc.
(7) If in any proceeding or as a condition precedent to any proceeding referred to in subsection (6) any order, consent or ruling is required under the law of a province to be made or given by the superior court of the province or by a judge or official of the court, a like order, consent or ruling may be made or given by the Federal Court or by a judge or official of the Federal Court and, when so made or given, has the same effect for the purposes of the proceeding as if it were made or given by the superior court of the province or by a judge or official of the court.

Presentation of documents
(8) If a memorial, or a document relating to it, is presented for recording, for the purpose of any proceeding referred to in subsection (6), to any official in the land, personal property or other registry system of a province, it is to be accepted for recording in the same manner and to the same extent as if the memorial or document were a document evidencing a judgment or an amount referred to in subsection (4) for the purpose of a like proceeding.

Access for recording
(9) If access is sought to any person, place or thing in a province for the purpose of recording a memorial, or a document relating to it, the access must be granted in the same manner and to the same extent as if the memorial or document were a document evidencing a judgment or an amount referred to in subsection (4) for the purpose of a like proceeding.

Evidence deemed to have been provided
(10) If a memorial or document is issued by the Federal Court or signed or certified by a judge or official of the Court, any affidavit, declaration or other evidence required under the law of the province to be provided with or to accompany the memorial or document in the proceeding is deemed to have been provided with or to have accompanied the memorial or document as so required.

Prohibition — sale, etc., without consent
(11) Despite any law of Canada or of a province, no sheriff or other person may, without the written consent of the Minister, sell or otherwise dispose of any property or publish any notice or otherwise advertise in respect of any sale or other disposition of any property pursuant to any process issued or protected interest created in any proceeding to collect an amount certified in a certificate, any interest on the amount and any costs.

Subsequent consent
(12) Despite subsection (11), if the Minister's consent is subsequently given, any property that would have been affected by a process or protected interest referred to in that subsection had the Minister's consent been given at the time the process was issued or the protected interest was created is bound, seized, attached, charged or otherwise affected as if that consent had been given at the time the process was issued or the protected interest was created, as the case may be.

Completion of notices, etc.
(13) If information required to be set out by any sheriff or other person in a minute, notice or document required to be completed for any purpose cannot, because of subsection (11), be so set out, the sheriff or other person must complete the minute, notice or document to the extent possible without that information and, when the consent of the Minister is given, a further minute, notice or

document setting out all the information is to be completed for the same purpose. The sheriff or other person is deemed to have complied with any law or rule of court requiring the information to be set out in the minute, notice or document.

Application for an order

(14) A sheriff or other person who is unable, because of subsection (11) or (13), to comply with any law or rule of court is bound by any order made by a judge of the Federal Court, on an

Secured claims

(15) A protected interest that is registered in accordance with subsection 87(1) of the Bankruptcy and Insolvency Act

(a) is secured by a security and that, subject to subsection 87(2) of that Act, ranks as a secured claim under that Act; and

(b) is referred to in paragraph 86(2)(a) of that Act.

Details in certificates and memorials

(16) Despite any law of Canada or of a province, in any certificate in respect of a debtor, in any memorial evidencing the certificate or in any writ or document issued for the purpose of collecting an amount certified, it is sufficient for all purposes

(a) to set out, as the amount payable by the debtor, the total of amounts payable by the debtor without setting out the separate amounts making up that total; and

(b) to refer to the rate of interest to be charged on the separate amounts making up the amount payable in general terms as interest at the rate prescribed under this Act applicable from time to time on amounts payable to the Receiver General, without indicating the specific rates of interest to be charged on each of the separate amounts or to be charged for any particular period of time.

Definitions

(17) The definitions in this subsection apply in this section.

memorial

protected interest

record

2001, c. 25, s. 58.

Detention of and lien on imported or exported goods

97.25 (1) Any goods reported for exportation under section 95 or imported by or on behalf of a debtor are subject to a lien for the amount owed by the debtor and may be detained by an officer at the expense of the debtor until that amount is paid.

Conveyances

(2) Any conveyance used for the importation of goods in respect of which a notice under section 109.3 has been served is subject to a lien for the amount owed by the debtor and may be detained by an officer at the expense of the person on whom the notice was served until the amount set out in the notice is paid.

Sale of detained goods

(3) Subject to the regulations, the Minister, on giving 30 days' notice in writing to the debtor at the debtor's latest known address, may direct that any good imported or reported for exportation by or on behalf of the debtor, or any conveyance, that has been detained be sold

(a) if the good is spirits or specially denatured alcohol, to a spirits licensee;

(b) if the good is wine, to a wine licensee;

(c) if the good is raw leaf tobacco or a tobacco product, to a tobacco licensee;

(d) if the good is a restricted formulation, to a licensed user; or

(e) in any other case, by public auction or public tender or by the Minister of Public Works and Government Services under the

Surplus Crown Assets Act

Excise stamps not to be sold

(3.1) Despite subsection (3), the Minister shall not direct that detained excise stamps be sold.

Proceeds of sale

(4) The proceeds of any sale shall be applied to amounts owed by the debtor, any expenses incurred

by Her Majesty in right of Canada in respect of the goods sold and any duties on the goods and the surplus, if any, shall be paid to the debtor.
2001, c. 25, s. 58;
2007, c. 18, s. 136;
2010, c. 12, s. 49.

Set-off
97.26 The Minister may require that an amount specified by the Minister be deducted from or set-off against an amount that is or may become payable to a debtor by Her Majesty in Right of Canada. If an amount payable to a person under a provision of this Act has at any time been deducted or set-off, the amount is deemed to have been paid to the debtor at that time under that provision and to have been paid by the debtor at that time on account of the debt to Her Majesty.
2001, c. 25, s. 58.

Refund may be applied against liabilities
97.27 The Minister of Public Safety and Emergency Preparedness may, if a person is or is about to become liable to make any payment to Her Majesty in right of Canada or in right of a province, apply the amount of any drawback, refund or relief granted under section 74 or 76 of this Act or section 89, 101 or 113 of the
Customs Tariff
2001, c. 25, s. 58;
2005, c. 38, ss. 84, 145.

Garnishment and Non-arm's Length Transfers

Garnishment — general
97.28 (1) If the Minister has knowledge or suspects that a person is or will be, within one year, liable to make a payment to a debtor, the Minister may, by notice in writing, require the person to pay without delay, if the moneys are immediately payable, and, in any other case, as and when the moneys become payable, the moneys otherwise payable to the debtor in whole or in part to the Receiver General on account of the debtor's liability under this Act.

Garnishment — institutions
(2) The Minister may, by notice in writing, require the following institutions or persons to pay in whole or in part to the Receiver General on account of a debtor's liability the moneys that would otherwise be loaned, advanced or paid if the Minister has knowledge or suspects that within ninety days
(a) a bank, credit union, trust company or other similar person (in this section referred to as the "institution") will loan or advance moneys to, or make a payment on behalf of, or make a payment in respect of a negotiable instrument issued by, a debtor who is indebted to the institution and who has granted security in respect of the indebtedness; or
(b) a person, other than an institution, will loan or advance moneys to, or make a payment on behalf of, a debtor who the Minister knows or suspects
(i) is employed by, or is engaged in providing services or property to, that person or was or will be, within ninety days, so employed or engaged, or
(ii) if that person is a corporation, is not dealing at arm's length with that person.
Any moneys so paid to the Receiver General are deemed to have been loaned, advanced or paid to the debtor.

Effect of receipt
(3) A receipt issued by the Minister for moneys paid as required under this section is a good and sufficient discharge of the original liability to the extent of the payment.

Periodic payments
(4) If the Minister has, under this section, required a person to pay to the Receiver General on account of the liability under this Act of a debtor moneys otherwise payable by the person to the debtor as interest, rent, remuneration, a dividend, an annuity or other periodic payment, the

requirement applies to all such payments to be made by the person to the debtor until the liability under this Act is satisfied, and operates to require payments to the Receiver General out of each such payment of such amount as is required by the Minister in a notice in writing.

Failure to comply

(5) Every person who fails to comply with a requirement under subsection (1) or (4) is liable to pay to Her Majesty in right of Canada an amount equal to the amount that the person was required under that subsection to pay to the Receiver General.

Failure to comply — institutions

(6) Every institution or person that fails to comply with a requirement under subsection (2) is liable to pay to Her Majesty in right of Canada an amount equal to the lesser of

(a) the total of moneys loaned, advanced or paid to the debtor, and

(b) the amount that the institution or person was required under that subsection to pay to the Receiver General.

Service

(7) If a person carries on business under a name or style other than the person's own name, notification to the person of a requirement under subsection (1) or (2) may be addressed to the name or style under which the person carries on business and, in the case of personal service, is validly served if it is left with an adult person employed at the place of business of the addressee.

Service — partnerships

(8) If persons carry on business in partnership, notification to the persons of a requirement under subsection (1) or (2) may be addressed to the partnership name and, in the case of personal service, is deemed to be validly served if it is served on one of the partners or left with an adult person employed at the place of business of the partnership.

Effect of payment as required

(9) If an amount that would otherwise have been payable to or on behalf of a debtor is paid by a person to the Receiver General pursuant to a notice served on the person under this section or pursuant to an assessment under section 97.44, the person is deemed, for all purposes, to have paid the amount to or on behalf of the debtor.

Application to Her Majesty in right of a province

(10) Provisions of this Part that provide that a person who has been required by the Minister to pay to the Receiver General an amount that would otherwise be loaned, advanced or paid to a debtor who is liable to make a payment under this Act apply to Her Majesty in right of a province.

2001, c. 25, s. 58.

Liability — non-arm's length transfers

97.29 (1) If a person transfers property, either directly or indirectly, by means of a trust or by any other means, to the transferor's spouse or common-law partner or an individual who has since become the transferor's spouse or common-law partner, an individual who was under eighteen years of age, or another person with whom the transferor was not dealing at arm's length, the transferee and transferor are jointly and severally or solidarily liable to pay an amount equal to the lesser of

(a) the amount determined by the formula

is the amount, if any, by which the fair market value of the property at the time of transfer exceeds the fair market value at that time of the consideration given by the transferee for the transfer of the property, and

is the amount, if any, by which the amount assessed the transferee under subsection 297(3) of the Excise Act, 2001

Excise Tax Act

Income Tax Act

(b) the total of all amounts each of which is

(i) an amount that the transferor is liable to pay under this Act, or

(ii) interest or a penalty for which the transferor is liable as of the time of transfer.

However, nothing in this subsection limits the liability of the transferor under any other provision of this Act.

Fair market value of undivided interest
(2) For the purpose of this section, the fair market value at any time of an undivided interest in a property, expressed as a proportionate interest in that property, is, subject to subsection (4), equal to the same proportion of the fair market value of that property at that time.
Rules applicable
(3) If a transferor and transferee have, under subsection (1), become jointly and severally or solidarily liable in respect of all or part of the liability of the transferor under this Act, the following rules apply:
(a) a payment by the transferee on account of the transferee's liability discharges, to the extent of the payment, the joint liability; and
(b) a payment by the transferor on account of the transferor's liability discharges the transferee's liability only to the extent that the payment operates to reduce the transferor's liability to an amount less than the amount in respect of which the transferee was made jointly and severally or solidarily liable.
Transfers to spouse or common-law partner
(4) Despite subsection (1), if at any time a debtor transfers property to the debtor's spouse or common-law partner under a decree, order or judgment of a competent tribunal or under a written separation agreement and, at that time, the debtor and the debtor's spouse or common-law partner were separated and living apart as a result of the breakdown of their marriage or common-law partnership (as defined in subsection 248(1) of the
Income Tax Act
Related persons
(5) For the purposes of this section,
(a) related persons are deemed not to deal with each other at arm's length, and it is a question of fact whether persons not related to each other were, at any particular time, dealing with each other at arm's length;
(b) persons are related to each other if they are related persons within the meaning of subsections 251(2) to (6) of the
Income Tax Act
(c) a member of a partnership is deemed to be related to the partnership.
Definitions
(6) The definitions in this subsection apply in this section.
common-law partner
Income Tax Act
common-law partnership
Income Tax Act
property
2001, c. 25, s. 58;
2002, c. 22, s. 408.

Acquisition of Property and Seizures

Acquisition of debtor's property
97.3 For the purpose of collecting amounts owed by a debtor, the Minister may purchase or otherwise acquire any interest in the debtor's property that the Minister is given a right to acquire in legal proceedings or under a court order or that is offered for sale or redemption, and may dispose of any interest so acquired in any manner that the Minister considers reasonable.
2001, c. 25, s. 58.
Moneys seized from debtor
97.31 (1) If the Minister has knowledge or suspects that a person is holding moneys that were seized by a police officer, in the course of administering or enforcing the criminal law of Canada, from a debtor and that are restorable to the debtor, the Minister may, by notice in writing, require that person

to turn over the moneys otherwise restorable to the debtor, in whole or in part, to the Receiver General on account of the debtor's liability under this Act.
Receipt
(2) A receipt issued for moneys turned over is a good and sufficient discharge of the requirement to restore the moneys to the debtor to the extent of the amount so turned over.
2001, c. 25, s. 58.
Seizure of chattels
97.32 (1) If a person fails to pay an amount as required under this Act, the Minister may give thirty days notice to the person by registered or certified mail addressed to the person at their latest known address of the Minister's intention to direct that the person's goods and chattels be seized and sold. If the person fails to make the payment before the expiration of the thirty days, the Minister may issue a certificate of the failure and direct that the person's goods and chattels be seized.
Sale of seized property
(2) Seized property must be kept for ten days at the expense and risk of the owner and, if the owner does not pay the amount due together with all expenses within the ten days, the property seized shall be sold by public auction.
Notice of sale
(3) Except in the case of perishable goods, notice of the sale setting out the time and place of the sale together with a general description of the property to be sold must be published, a reasonable time before the goods are sold, in one or more newspapers of general local circulation.
Surplus
(4) Any surplus resulting from a sale, after deduction of the amount owing and all expenses, must be paid or returned to the owner of the property seized.
Exemption from seizure
(5) Goods and chattels of any person that would be exempt from seizure under a writ of execution issued out of a superior court of the province in which the seizure is made are exempt from seizure under this section.
2001, c. 25, s. 58.
Person leaving Canada
97.33 (1) If the Minister suspects that a person who is liable to pay an amount under this Act or would be so liable if the time for payment of the amount had arrived has left or is about to leave Canada, the Minister may, before the day otherwise fixed for payment, by notice in writing, demand payment of the amount. Despite any other provision of this Act, the person shall pay the amount immediately.
Failure to pay
(2) If a person fails to pay an amount as required, the Minister may direct that the goods and chattels of the person be seized and subsections 97.32(2) to (5) apply.
2001, c. 25, s. 58.

Collection Restrictions

Collection action delayed
97.34 (1) If a person is liable for the payment of an amount under this Act, if an amount is demanded in a notice served under section 109.3 or 124, or if an amount is demanded under paragraph 133(1)(c) or subsection 133(1.1) in a notice served under subsection 131(2), the Minister must not, for the purpose of collecting the amount, take the following actions until the ninety-first day after the day notice is given to the debtor:
(a) commence legal proceedings in a court;
(b) certify the amount under section 97.24;
(c) require the retention of the amount by way of deduction or set-off under section 97.26;
(d) require a person or institution to make a payment under section 97.28;
(e) require a person to turn over moneys under subsection 97.31(1); or

(f) give a notice, issue a certificate or make a direction under subsection 97.32(1).
Appeal to Federal Court
(2) If a person has appealed a decision of the Minister of Public Safety and Emergency Preparedness to the Federal Court under section 97.23 or 135, the Minister must not take any action described in subsection (1) to collect the amount in controversy before the date of the decision of the Court or the day on which the person discontinues the appeal.
Reference to Canadian International Trade Tribunal
(3) If the President has referred a question to the Canadian International Trade Tribunal under section 70, the Minister must not take any action described in subsection (1) to collect the amount in controversy before the day on which the question is determined by the Tribunal.
Effect of appeal
(4) If a person has made a request under section 60 or 129 or has appealed under section 67 or 68 and the person agrees in writing with the Minister of Public Safety and Emergency Preparedness to delay proceedings on the request or appeal, as the case may be, until judgment has been given in another action before the Federal Court, the Canadian International Trade Tribunal or the Supreme Court of Canada, in which action the issue is the same or substantially the same as that raised in the request or appeal of the person, the Minister may take any of the actions described in subsection (1) for the purpose of collecting the amount payable, or a part of the amount payable, determined in a manner consistent with the decision or judgment in the other action at any time after the Minister of Public Safety and Emergency Preparedness notifies the person in writing that
(a) the decision of the Canadian International Trade Tribunal or Federal Court in that action has been mailed to the Minister of Public Safety and Emergency Preparedness;
(b) judgment has been pronounced by the Federal Court of Appeal in that action; or
(c) judgment has been delivered by the Supreme Court of Canada in that action.
Effect of taking security
(5) The Minister must not, for the purpose of collecting an amount payable, or a part of an amount payable, under this Act, take any of the actions described in subsection (1) if a person has given security to the Minister of Public Safety and Emergency Preparedness when requesting or appealing from a decision of that Minister or the President.
2001, c. 25, s. 58;
2002, c. 8, s. 193;
2005, c. 38, ss. 78, 85, 145.
Authorization to proceed immediately
97.35 (1) Despite section 97.34, if, on
Notice not sent
(2) An authorization may be granted by a judge notwithstanding that a notice in respect of the amount has not been sent to the debtor at or before the time the application is made if the judge is satisfied that the receipt of the notice by the debtor would likely further jeopardize the collection of the amount and, for the purposes of sections 97.22, 97.24, 97.26, 97.28, 97.31 and 97.32, the amount in respect of which an authorization is granted is deemed to be an amount payable under this Act.
Affidavits
(3) Statements contained in an affidavit filed in the context of an application made under this section may be based on belief but must include the grounds for the belief.
Service of authorization
(4) An authorization must be served by the Minister on the debtor within 72 hours after it is granted, except if the judge orders the authorization to be served at some other time specified in the authorization, and, if a notice has not been sent to the debtor at or before the time of the application, the notice is to be served together with the authorization.
How service effected
(5) Service on a debtor must be effected by personal service or in accordance with the directions of a judge.
Application to judge for direction

(6) If service on a debtor cannot reasonably otherwise be effected as and when required under this section, the Minister may, as soon as is practicable, apply to a judge for further direction.
Review of authorization
(7) If a judge of a court has granted an authorization, the debtor may, on six clear days notice to the Deputy Attorney General of Canada, apply to a judge of the court to review the authorization.
Limitation period for review application
(8) An application under subsection (7) must be made
(a) within thirty days after the day on which the authorization was served on the debtor in accordance with this section; or
(b) within any further time that a judge may allow, on being satisfied that the application was made as soon as was practicable.
Hearing
(9) An application may, on request of the debtor, be heard
Disposition of application
(10) On an application, the judge is to determine the question summarily and may confirm, set aside or vary the authorization and make any other order that the judge considers appropriate.
Directions
(11) If any question arises as to the course to be followed in connection with anything done or being done under this section and there is no direction in this section in respect of the matter, a judge may give any direction in respect of the matter that, in the opinion of the judge, is appropriate.
No appeal from review order
(12) No appeal lies from an order of a judge made under subsection (10).
2001, c. 25, s. 58.

Trustees, Receivers and Personal Representatives

Bankruptcies
97.36 (1) The following rules apply to a person who is a bankrupt:
(a) the trustee in bankruptcy is the agent of the bankrupt and any act performed by the trustee in the administration of the estate of the bankrupt or in the carrying on of any business of the bankrupt is deemed to have been made by the trustee as agent of the bankrupt;
(b) the estate of the bankrupt is not a trust or an estate;
(c) the property and money of the bankrupt immediately before the day of the bankruptcy does not pass to or vest in the trustee in bankruptcy on the bankruptcy order being made or the assignment in bankruptcy being filed but remains vested in the bankrupt;
(d) the trustee in bankruptcy, and not the bankrupt, is liable for the payment of all amounts (other than amounts that relate solely to activities in which the bankrupt begins to engage on or after the day of the bankruptcy and to which the bankruptcy does not relate) that become payable by the bankrupt under this Act during the period beginning on the day immediately after the day the trustee became the trustee in bankruptcy of the bankrupt and ending on the day the discharge of the trustee is granted under the
Bankruptcy and Insolvency Act
(i) the trustee is liable for the payment of amounts that became payable by the bankrupt after the day of the bankruptcy only to the extent of the property and money of the bankrupt in possession of the trustee available to satisfy the liability, and
(ii) the trustee is not liable for the payment of any amount for which a receiver is liable under section 97.37,
(e) if, on or after the day of bankruptcy, the bankrupt begins to engage in particular activities to which the bankruptcy does not relate, the particular activities are deemed to be separate from the activities of the person to which the bankruptcy relates as though the particular activities were activities of a separate person;
(f) subject to paragraph (h), the trustee in bankruptcy shall perform all the obligations under this Act

of the bankrupt in respect of the activities of the bankrupt to which the bankruptcy relates for the period beginning on the day immediately after the day of bankruptcy and ending on the day the discharge of the trustee is granted under the
Bankruptcy and Insolvency Act
(g) subject to paragraph (h), if the bankrupt has not on or before the day of bankruptcy fulfilled all of their obligations under this Act in respect of any activities of the bankrupt on or before the day of bankruptcy, the trustee in bankruptcy shall fulfil those obligations, unless the Minister waives in writing the requirement for the trustee to do so;
(h) if there is a receiver with authority in respect of a business, a property, affairs or assets of the bankrupt, the trustee in bankruptcy is not required to perform the obligations of the bankrupt under this Act to the extent that the receiver is required under section 97.37 to perform those obligations; and
(i) the property and money held by the trustee in bankruptcy for the bankrupt on the day an order of absolute discharge of the bankrupt is granted under the
Bankruptcy and Insolvency Act

Definition of
bankrupt
(2) In this section,
bankrupt
Bankruptcy and Insolvency Act
2001, c. 25, s. 58;
2004, c. 25, s. 196.

Definitions
97.37 (1) The definitions in this subsection apply in this section.
business
relevant assets
(a) if the receiver's authority relates to all the properties, businesses, affairs and assets of a person, all those properties, businesses, affairs and assets; and
(b) if the receiver's authority relates to only part of the properties, businesses, affairs or assets of a person, that part of the properties, businesses, affairs or assets, as the case may be.

Receivers
(2) The following rules apply to a receiver who on a particular day is vested with the authority to manage, operate, liquidate or wind up any business or property, or to manage and care for the affairs and assets, of a person:
(a) the receiver is an agent of the person and any act performed by the receiver in respect of the relevant assets of the receiver is deemed to have been performed, as the case may be, by the receiver as agent on behalf of the person;
(b) the receiver is not a trustee of the estate of the person or any part of the estate of the person;
(c) if the relevant assets of the receiver are a part and not all of the person's businesses, properties, affairs or assets, the relevant assets of the receiver are deemed to be, throughout the period during which the receiver is acting as receiver of the person, separate from the remainder of the businesses, properties, affairs or assets of the person as though the relevant assets were businesses, properties, affairs or assets, as the case may be, of a separate person;
(d) the person and the receiver are jointly and severally or solidarily liable for the payment of all amounts that become payable by the person under this Act before or during the period during which the receiver is acting as receiver of the person to the extent that the amounts can reasonably be considered to relate to the relevant assets of the receiver or to the businesses, properties, affairs or assets of the person that would have been the relevant assets of the receiver if the receiver had been acting as receiver of the person at the time the amounts became payable except that
(i) the receiver is liable for the payment of amounts that became payable before that period only to the extent of the property and money of the person in possession or under the control and management of the receiver after

(A) satisfying the claims of creditors whose claims ranked, on the particular day, in priority to the claim of the Crown in respect of the amounts, and

(B) paying any amounts that the receiver is required to pay to a trustee in bankruptcy of the person, and

(ii) the payment by the person or the receiver of an amount in respect of the liability discharges the joint liability to the extent of that amount;

(e) the receiver shall perform all the obligations, in respect of the relevant assets of the receiver for the period during which the receiver is acting as receiver, that are required under this Act to be performed by the person, as if the relevant assets were the only properties, businesses, affairs and assets of the person; and

(f) if the person has not on or before the particular day fulfilled their obligations under this Act before the period during which the receiver was acting as receiver, the receiver shall fulfil those obligations for that period that relate to the businesses, properties, affairs or assets of the person that would have been the relevant assets of the receiver if the receiver had been acting as receiver of the person during that period, unless the Minister waives in writing the requirement for the receiver to do so.

2001, c. 25, s. 58.

Definitions

97.38 (1) The definitions in this subsection apply in this section and in section 97.39.

trust

trustee

Trustee's liability

(2) Subject to subsection (3), each trustee of a trust is liable to satisfy every obligation imposed on the trust under this Act, whether the obligation was imposed during or before the period during which the trustee acts as trustee of the trust, but the satisfaction of an obligation of a trust by one of the trustees of the trust discharges the liability of all other trustees of the trust to satisfy that obligation.

Joint and several or solidary liability

(3) A trustee of a trust is jointly and severally or solidarily liable with the trust and each of the other trustees, if any, for the payment of all amounts that become payable by the trust under this Act before or during the period during which the trustee acts as trustee of the trust except that

(a) the trustee is liable for the payment of amounts that became payable before that period only to the extent of the property and money of the trust under the control of the trustee; and

(b) the payment by the trust or the trustee of an amount in respect of the liability discharges the joint liability to the extent of that amount.

Waiver

(4) The Minister may, in writing, waive the requirement for the personal representative of a deceased individual to fulfil the obligations under this Act in respect of the activities of the deceased individual that occurred on or before the day the individual died.

Activities of a trustee

(5) For the purposes of this Act, if a person acts as trustee of a trust, anything done by the person in the person's capacity as trustee of the trust is deemed to have been done by the trust and not by the person.

2001, c. 25, s. 58.

Definition of

representative

97.39 (1) In this section,

representative

Certificates for receivers

(2) Every receiver shall, before distributing to any person any property or money under the control of the receiver in the receiver's capacity as receiver, obtain a certificate from the Minister certifying that the following amounts have been paid or security for the payment of the amounts has been accepted

by the Minister:

(a) amounts that the person is or can reasonably be expected to become liable to pay under this Act at or before the time the distribution is made; and

(b) amounts that the receiver is or can reasonably be expected to become liable to pay in the receiver's capacity as receiver.

Certificates for representatives

(3) Every representative shall, before distributing to any person any property or money under the control of the representative in the representative's capacity as representative, obtain a certificate from the Minister certifying that the following amounts have been paid or that security for the payment of the amounts has been accepted by the Minister:

(a) amounts that the person is or can reasonably be expected to become liable to pay under this Act at or before the time the distribution is made; and

(b) amounts that the representative is or can reasonably be expected to become liable to pay in the representative's capacity as representative.

Liability for failure to obtain certificate

(4) Any receiver or representative who distributes property or money without obtaining a certificate in respect of the amounts referred to in subsection (2) or (3) is personally liable for the payment of those amounts to the extent of the value of the property or money so distributed.

2001, c. 25, s. 58.

Amalgamations and Windings-up

Amalgamations

97.4 (1) If two or more corporations (in this section each referred to as a "predecessor") are merged or amalgamated to form one corporation (in this section referred to as the "new corporation"), the new corporation is, for the purposes of this Act, deemed to be a separate person from each of the predecessors and the same corporation as, and a continuation of, each predecessor.

Exception

(2) Subsection (1) does not apply to the merger or amalgamation of two or more corporations that is the result of the acquisition of property of one corporation by another corporation pursuant to the purchase of the property by the other corporation or as the result of the distribution of the property to the other corporation on the winding-up of the corporation.

2001, c. 25, s. 58.

Winding-up

97.41 For the purposes of this Act, if at any time a particular corporation is wound up and not less than 90% of the issued shares of each class of the capital stock of the particular corporation were, immediately before that time, owned by another corporation, the other corporation is deemed to be the same corporation as, and a continuation of, the particular corporation.

2001, c. 25, s. 58.

Partnerships

Partnerships

97.42 (1) For the purposes of this Act, anything done by a person as a member of a partnership is deemed to have been done by the partnership in the course of the partnership's activities and not to have been done by the person.

Joint and several or solidary liability

(2) A partnership and each member or former member (each of which is referred to in this subsection as the "member") of the partnership (other than a member which is a limited partner and is not a general partner) are jointly and severally or solidarily liable for

(a) the payment of all amounts that become payable by the partnership under this Act before or during the period during which the member is a member of the partnership or, if the member was a

member of the partnership at the time the partnership was dissolved, after the dissolution of the partnership, except that
(i) the member is liable for the payment of amounts that become payable before that period only to the extent of the property and money that is regarded as property or money of the partnership in accordance with the laws of the province governing the partnership, and
(ii) the payment by the partnership or by any member of the partnership of an amount in respect of the liability discharges the joint liability to the extent of that amount; and
(b) all other obligations under this Act that arose before or during the period for which the partnership is liable or, if the member was a member of the partnership at the time the partnership was dissolved, the obligations that arose upon or as a consequence of the dissolution.
2001, c. 25, s. 58.

Unincorporated Bodies

Compliance by unincorporated bodies
97.43 If any amount is required to be paid or any other thing is required to be done under this Act by a person (in this section referred to as the "body") that is not an individual, corporation, partnership, trust or estate, the following persons are jointly and severally or solidarily liable to pay that amount or to comply with the requirement:
(a) every member of the body holding office as president, chairperson, treasurer, secretary or similar officer of the body;
(b) if there are no members referred to in paragraph (a), every member of any committee having management of the affairs of the body; and
(c) if there are no members referred to in paragraph (a) or (b), every member of the body.
The payment of the amount or the fullfilment of the requirement by a member is deemed to be compliance with the requirement.
2001, c. 25, s. 58.

Assessments, Objections and Appeals

Assessments

Assessments — garnishments and non-arms length transfers
97.44 (1) The Minister may assess any amount that a person is liable to pay
(a) under section 97.28, before the expiry of four years after the notice from the Minister requiring the payment is issued to the person; and
(b) under section 97.29, at any time.
The Minister may reassess the amount or make an additional assessment.
Interest
(2) If a person has been assessed an amount under subsection (1), the person shall pay, in addition to the amount, interest at the prescribed rate for the period beginning on the first day after the day the amount was assessed and ending on the day the amount is paid.
Exception
(3) Paragraph (1)(a) does not apply in respect of a reassessment of a person made
(a) to give effect to a decision on an objection or appeal; or
(b) with the consent in writing of the person to dispose of an appeal.
When assessment may be made
(4) An assessment under paragraph (1)(a) may be made at any time if the person to be assessed has
(a) made a misrepresentation that is attributable to the person's neglect, carelessness or wilful default;
(b) committed fraud in supplying, or failing to supply, any information under this Act; or
(c) filed a waiver under subsection (5) that is in effect at that time.

Waiver
(5) Any person may, within the time otherwise limited by paragraph (1)(a) for assessing the person, waive the application of that paragraph by filing with the Minister a waiver in the prescribed form specifying the matter in respect of which the person waives the application of that paragraph.
Revoking waiver
(6) Any person who files a waiver may revoke the waiver on six months notice to the Minister by filing with the Minister a notice of revocation of the waiver in the prescribed form.
2001, c. 25, s. 58.
Liability not affected
97.45 (1) Liability under this Part to pay any amount is not affected by an incorrect or incomplete assessment or by the fact that no assessment has been made.
Assessment deemed valid
(2) Subject to being reassessed or vacated as a result of an objection or appeal under this Part, an assessment is valid and binding, despite any error, defect or omission in the assessment or in any proceeding under this Part relating to it.
Irregularities
(3) An appeal from an assessment must not be allowed by reason only of an irregularity, informality, omission or error on the part of any person in the observation of any directory provision of this Part.
2001, c. 25, s. 58.
Notice of assessment
97.46 After making an assessment, the Minister must send to the person assessed a notice of assessment.
2001, c. 25, s. 58.
Assessment before collection
97.47 (1) The Minister may not collect an amount under section 97.44 unless that amount has been assessed.
Payment of remainder
(2) An amount that is unpaid by a person and the subject of a notice of assessment is payable immediately by the person to the Receiver General.
Security if objection or appeal
(3) If a person objects to or appeals from an assessment under this Part, the Minister shall accept security, in an amount and a form satisfactory to the Minister, given by or on behalf of the person, for the payment of any amount that is in controversy.
2001, c. 25, s. 58.

Objections and Appeals

Objection to assessment
97.48 (1) Any person who has been assessed under section 97.44 and who objects to the assessment may, within ninety days after the day notice of the assessment is sent to the person, file with the Minister a notice of objection in the prescribed form and manner setting out the reasons for the objection and all relevant facts.
Issues to be decided
(2) If a person objects to an assessment, the notice of objection must
(a) reasonably describe each issue to be decided;
(b) specify in respect of each issue the relief sought, expressed as the change in any amount that is relevant for the purposes of the assessment; and
(c) provide the facts and reasons relied on by the person in respect of each issue.
Late compliance
(3) If a notice of objection filed by a person to whom subsection (2) applies does not include the information required by paragraph (2)(b) or (c) in respect of an issue to be decided that is described in the notice, the Minister may in writing request the person to provide the information, and those

paragraphs are deemed to have been complied with in respect of the issue if, within 60 days after the request is made, the person submits the information in writing to the Minister.
Limitation on objections
(4) If a person has filed a notice of objection to an assessment and the Minister makes a particular assessment under subsection (8) pursuant to the notice of objection or in accordance with an order of a court vacating, varying or restoring an assessment or referring an assessment back to the Minister for reconsideration and reassessment, the person may object to the particular assessment in respect of an issue
(a) only if the person complied with subsection (2) in the notice with respect to that issue; and
(b) only with respect to the relief sought in respect of that issue as specified by the person in the notice.
Application of subsection (4)
(5) If a person has filed a notice of objection to an assessment (in this subsection referred to as the "earlier assessment") and the Minister makes a particular assessment under subsection (8) pursuant to the notice of objection, subsection (4) does not limit the right of the person to object to the particular assessment in respect of an issue that was part of the particular assessment and not a part of the earlier assessment.
Limitation on objections
(6) Despite subsection (1), no objection may be made by a person in respect of an issue for which the right of objection has been waived in writing by the person.
Acceptance of objection
(7) The Minister may accept a notice of objection even if it was not filed in the prescribed manner.
Consideration of objection
(8) On receipt of a notice of objection, the Minister must, without delay, reconsider the assessment and vacate or confirm the assessment or make a reassessment.
Waiving reconsideration
(9) If, in a notice of objection, a person who wishes to appeal directly to the Tax Court of Canada requests the Minister not to reconsider the assessment objected to, the Minister may confirm the assessment without reconsideration.
Notice of decision
(10) After reconsidering or confirming an assessment, the Minister must send to the person objecting a notice of the Minister's decision by registered or certified mail.
2001, c. 25, s. 58.
Appeal to the Tax Court of Canada
97.49 If a person files a notice of objection to an assessment and the Minister sends to the person a notice of a reassessment or an additional assessment, in respect of any matter dealt with in the notice of objection, the person may, within ninety days after the day the notice of reassessment or additional assessment was sent by the Minister,
(a) appeal to the Tax Court of Canada; or
(b) if an appeal has already been instituted in respect of the matter, amend the appeal by joining to it an appeal in respect of the reassessment or additional assessment in any manner and on any terms that the Court directs.
2001, c. 25, s. 58.
Extension of time by Minister
97.5 (1) If no objection to an assessment is filed under section 97.48, within the time limit otherwise provided, a person may make an application to the Minister to extend the time for filing a notice of objection and the Minister may grant the application.
Contents of application
(2) The application must set out the reasons why the notice of objection was not filed within the time otherwise limited by this Part for doing so.
How application made
(3) The application must be made by delivering or mailing the application and a copy of the notice of

objection to the Chief of Appeals in a Tax Services Office or Taxation Centre of the Canada Revenue Agency.
Exception
(4) The Minister may accept the application even if it was not delivered or mailed to the person or place specified in subsection (3).
Duties of Minister
(5) On receipt of the application, the Minister must, without delay, consider it, and notify the person of his or her decision by registered or certified mail.
Date of objection if application granted
(6) If the application is granted, the notice of objection is deemed to have been filed on the day the decision of the Minister is mailed to the person.
When order to be made
(7) No application may be granted under this section unless
(a) the application is made within one year after the expiration of the time otherwise limited by this Part for objecting; and
(b) the person demonstrates that
(i) within the time otherwise limited by this Part for objecting, the person was unable to act or to give a mandate to act in the person's name, or the person had a
(ii) it would be just and equitable to grant the application, and
(iii) the application was made as soon as circumstances permitted.
2001, c. 25, s. 58;
2005, c. 38, s. 79.
Extension of time by Tax Court of Canada
97.51 (1) A person who has made an application under section 97.5 may apply to the Tax Court of Canada to have the application granted after either
(a) the Minister has refused the application; or
(b) ninety days have elapsed after service of the application and the Minister has not notified the person of the Minister's decision.
If paragraph (a) applies, the application under this subsection must be made within thirty days after the application is refused.
How application made
(2) The application must be made by filing in the Registry of the Tax Court of Canada, in accordance with the provisions of the
Tax Court of Canada Act
Copy to the Commissioner
(3) After receiving the application, the Tax Court of Canada must send a copy of it to the office of the Commissioner.
Powers of Court
(4) The Tax Court of Canada may dispose of the application by dismissing or granting it. If the Court grants the application, it may impose any terms that it considers just or order that the notice of objection be deemed to be a valid objection as of the date of the order.
When application to be granted
(5) No application may be granted under this section unless
(a) the application was made under subsection 97.5(1) within one year after the expiration of the time set out in this Part for objecting; and
(b) the person demonstrates that
(i) within the time otherwise limited by this Part for objecting, the person was unable to act or to give a mandate to act in the person's name, or the person had a
(ii) it would be just and equitable to grant the application, and
(iii) the application was made under subsection 97.5(1) as soon as circumstances permitted.
2001, c. 25, s. 58.
Extension of time to appeal

97.52 (1) If no appeal to the Tax Court of Canada has been taken under section 97.53 within the time set out in that section, a person may make an application to the Court for an order extending the time within which an appeal may be made, and the Court may make an order extending the time for appealing and may impose any terms that it considers just.

Contents of application

(2) The application must set out the reasons why the appeal was not taken on time.

How application made

(3) The application must be made by filing in the Registry of the Tax Court of Canada, in accordance with the
Tax Court of Canada Act

Copy to Deputy Attorney General of Canada

(4) After receiving the application, the Tax Court of Canada must send a copy of the application to the office of the Deputy Attorney General of Canada.

When order to be made

(5) No order may be made under this section unless
(a) the application was made within one year after the expiration of the time otherwise limited by this Part for appealing; and
(b) the person demonstrates that
(i) within the time otherwise limited by this Part for appealing, the person was unable to act or to give a mandate to act in the person's name, or the person had a
(ii) it would be just and equitable to grant the application,
(iii) the application was made as soon as circumstances permitted, and
(iv) there are reasonable grounds for appealing from an assessment.
2001, c. 25, s. 58.

Appeal

97.53 A person who has filed a notice of objection to an assessment under this Part may appeal to the Tax Court of Canada to have the assessment vacated or a reassessment made after either
(a) the Minister has confirmed the assessment or has reassessed; or
(b) 180 days have elapsed after the filing of the notice of objection and the Minister has not notified the person that the Minister has vacated or confirmed the assessment or has reassessed.
If paragraph (a) applies, an application to appeal under this section must be made within ninety days after the day notice is sent to the person under subsection 97.48(10).
2001, c. 25, s. 58.

Limitation on appeals to the Tax Court of Canada

97.54 (1) Despite section 97.49 and 97.53, a person may appeal to the Tax Court of Canada only with respect to
(a) an issue in respect of which the person has complied with subsection 97.48(2) in the notice of objection; or
(b) an issue described in subsection 97.48(5) if the person was not required to file a notice of objection to the assessment that gave rise to the issue.
If paragraph (a) applies, the person may appeal only with respect to the relief sought in respect of the issue specified by the person in the notice.

No right of appeal

(2) Despite sections 97.49 and 97.53, a person may not appeal to the Tax Court of Canada to have an assessment vacated or varied in respect of an issue for which the right of objection or appeal has been waived in writing by the person.
2001, c. 25, s. 58.

Institution of appeal

97.55 An appeal to the Tax Court of Canada under this Part, other than one referred to in section 18.3001 of the
Tax Court of Canada Act
2001, c. 25, s. 58.

Notice to Commissioner
97.56 (1) If an appeal referred to in section 18.3001 of the
Tax Court of Canada Act
Notice, etc., forwarded to Tax Court of Canada
(2) Immediately after receiving notice of an appeal, the Commissioner must forward to the Tax Court of Canada and the appellant copies of all applications, notices of assessment, notices of objection and notifications, if any, that are relevant to the appeal. Once forwarded, the copies form part of the record before the Tax Court of Canada and are evidence of the existence of the documents and of the making of the statements contained in them.
2001, c. 25, s. 58.
Disposition of appeal
97.57 The Tax Court of Canada may dispose of an appeal from an assessment by dismissing or allowing it. If the appeal is allowed, the Court may vacate the assessment or refer it back to the Minister for reconsideration and reassessment.
2001, c. 25, s. 58.
References to Tax Court of Canada
97.58 (1) If the Minister and another person agree in writing that a question arising under this Part, in respect of any assessment or proposed assessment, should be determined by the Tax Court of Canada, that question shall be determined by that Court.
Time during consideration not to count
(2) The time between the day proceedings are taken in the Tax Court of Canada to have a question determined and the day the question is finally determined must not be counted in the calculation of
(a) the four-year period referred to in paragraph 97.44(1)(a);
(b) the time for service of a notice of objection to an assessment under section 97.48; or
(c) the time within which an appeal may be instituted under section 97.53.
2001, c. 25, s. 58.

PART VI

PART VI
Enforcement

Powers of Officers

Search of the person
98 (1) An officer may search
(a) any person who has arrived in Canada, within a reasonable time after his arrival in Canada,
(b) any person who is about to leave Canada, at any time prior to his departure, or
(c) any person who has had access to an area designated for use by persons about to leave Canada and who leaves the area but does not leave Canada, within a reasonable time after he leaves the area,
if the officer suspects on reasonable grounds that the person has secreted on or about his person anything in respect of which this Act has been or might be contravened, anything that would afford evidence with respect to a contravention of this Act or any goods the importation or exportation of which is prohibited, controlled or regulated under this or any other Act of Parliament.
Person taken before senior officer
(2) An officer who is about to search a person under this section shall, on the request of that person, forthwith take him before the senior officer at the place where the search is to take place.
Idem
(3) A senior officer before whom a person is taken pursuant to subsection (2) shall, if he sees no reasonable grounds for the search, discharge the person or, if he believes otherwise, direct that the person be searched.
Search by same sex

(4) No person shall be searched under this section by a person who is not of the same sex, and if there is no officer of the same sex at the place at which the search is to take place, an officer may authorize any suitable person of the same sex to perform the search.

Examination of goods

99 (1) An officer may

(a) at any time up to the time of release, examine any goods that have been imported and open or cause to be opened any package or container of imported goods and take samples of imported goods in reasonable amounts;

(b) at any time up to the time of release, examine any mail that has been imported and, subject to this section, open or cause to be opened any such mail that the officer suspects on reasonable grounds contains any goods referred to in the
Customs Tariff

(c) at any time up to the time of exportation, examine any goods that have been reported under section 95 and open or cause to be opened any package or container of such goods and take samples of such goods in reasonable amounts;

(c.1) at any time up to the time of exportation, examine any mail that is to be exported and, subject to this section, open or cause to be opened any such mail that the officer suspects on reasonable grounds contains any goods the exportation of which is prohibited, controlled or regulated under any Act of Parliament, and take samples of anything contained in such mail in reasonable amounts;

(d) where the officer suspects on reasonable grounds that an error has been made in the tariff classification, value for duty or quantity of any goods accounted for under section 32, or where a refund or drawback is requested in respect of any goods under this Act or pursuant to the
Customs Tariff

(d.1) where the officer suspects on reasonable grounds that an error has been made with respect to the origin claimed or determined for any goods accounted for under section 32, examine the goods and take samples thereof in reasonable amounts;

(e) where the officer suspects on reasonable grounds that this Act or the regulations or any other Act of Parliament administered or enforced by him or any regulations thereunder have been or might be contravened in respect of any goods, examine the goods and open or cause to be opened any package or container thereof; or

(f) where the officer suspects on reasonable grounds that this Act or the regulations or any other Act of Parliament administered or enforced by him or any regulations thereunder have been or might be contravened in respect of any conveyance or any goods thereon, stop, board and search the conveyance, examine any goods thereon and open or cause to be opened any package or container thereof and direct that the conveyance be moved to a customs office or other suitable place for any such search, examination or opening.

(2) and (3) Samples

(4) Samples taken pursuant to subsection (1) shall be disposed of in such manner as the Minister may direct.

R.S., 1985, c. 1 (2nd Supp.), s. 99;

1988, c. 65, s. 79;

2001, c. 25, s. 59;

2017, c. 7, s. 52.

Power to stop

99.1 (1) If an officer has reasonable grounds to suspect that a person has entered Canada without presenting himself or herself in accordance with subsection 11(1), the officer may stop that person within a reasonable time after the person has entered Canada.

Powers of officer

(2) An officer who stops a person referred to in subsection (1) may

(a) question the person; and

(b) in respect of goods imported by that person, examine them, cause to be opened any package or container of the imported goods and take samples of them in reasonable amounts.

2001, c. 25, s. 60.
Search of persons
99.2 (1) An officer may search any person who is in or is leaving a customs controlled area, other than a prescribed person or a member of a prescribed class of persons who may be searched under subsection (2), if the officer suspects on reasonable grounds that the person has secreted on or about their person anything in respect of which this Act or the regulations have been or might be contravened, anything that would afford evidence with respect to a contravention of this Act or the regulations or any goods the importation or exportation of which is prohibited, controlled or regulated under this or any other Act of Parliament.
Search of prescribed persons
(2) An officer may, in accordance with the regulations, search any prescribed person or member of a prescribed class of persons who is in or is leaving a customs controlled area.
Person taken before senior officer
(3) An officer who is about to search a person under this section shall, on the request of the person, immediately take that person before the senior officer at the place where the search is to be conducted.
Review by senior officer
(4) A senior officer before whom a person is taken by an officer shall, if the senior officer agrees with the officer that under subsection (1) or (2), as the case may be, the person may be searched, direct that the person be searched or, if the senior officer does not so agree, discharge the person.
Limitations on searches
(5) No person may be searched by an officer who is not of the same sex and, if there is no officer of the same sex at the place at which the search is to be conducted, an officer may authorize any suitable person of the same sex to conduct the search.
2001, c. 25, s. 60;
2009, c. 10, s. 10.
Non-intrusive examination of goods
99.3 (1) An officer may, in accordance with the regulations and without individualized suspicion, conduct a non-intrusive examination of goods in the custody or possession of a person who is in or is leaving a customs controlled area.
Other examination of goods
(2) An officer may examine any goods in the custody or possession of a person who is in or is leaving a customs controlled area and open or cause to be opened any baggage, package or container and take samples of the goods in reasonable amounts, if the officer suspects on reasonable grounds that this Act or any other Act of Parliament administered or enforced by the officer or any regulations made under it have been or might be contravened in respect of the goods.
Examination of abandoned goods
(3) An officer may, at any time, open or cause to be opened, examine and detain any goods, baggage, package or container that is found abandoned or that is not in the possession of any person in a customs controlled area.
2001, c. 25, s. 60;
2009, c. 10, s. 11.
Regulations
99.4 The Governor in Council may make regulations
(a) prescribing persons or classes of persons who may be searched under subsection 99.2(2);
(b) respecting, for the purposes of subsection 99.2(2), the circumstances and manner in which searches are to be conducted and the types of searches that may be conducted; and
(c) respecting, for the purposes of subsection 99.3(1), the manner in which examinations are to be conducted and the machines, instruments, devices or other apparatuses or classes of machines, instruments, devices or apparatuses that may be used to conduct examinations.
2001, c. 25, s. 60.
Powers of officer — mixed-traffic corridor

99.5 If an officer has reasonable grounds to suspect that a person, having stated under section 11.7 that they arrived from a location within Canada, did in fact arrive from a location outside Canada, the officer may
(a) question the person; and
(b) examine any goods carried by the person, cause any package or container of the goods to be opened and take samples of the goods in reasonable amounts.
2012, c. 19, s. 482.

Officer stationed on board conveyance
100 (1) An officer may be stationed on board any conveyance that has arrived in Canada from a place outside Canada for the purpose of doing anything he is required or authorized to do in the administration or enforcement of this or any other Act of Parliament.

Carriage, accommodation and food provided
(2) An officer stationed on board a conveyance pursuant to subsection (1) shall be carried free of charge, and the person in charge of the conveyance shall ensure that the officer is provided with suitable accommodation and food.

Detention of controlled goods
101 Goods that have been imported or are about to be exported may be detained by an officer until he is satisfied that the goods have been dealt with in accordance with this Act, and any other Act of Parliament that prohibits, controls or regulates the importation or exportation of goods, and any regulations made thereunder.

Disposition of goods illegally imported
102 (1) Goods that have been imported in contravention of this or any other Act of Parliament, or any regulation made thereunder, and that have been detained under section 101 shall be disposed of in accordance with that Act or regulation, but, where there is no provision in that Act or regulation for the disposition of such goods, the importer may abandon the goods to Her Majesty in right of Canada in accordance with section 36 or export them.

Idem
(2) Goods referred to in subsection (1) that are not disposed of, abandoned or exported in accordance with that subsection within such period of time as may be prescribed, may be deposited in a place of safe-keeping referred to in section 37 and, if they are so deposited, sections 37 to 39 apply in respect of the goods as if they had been deposited therein pursuant to section 37.

Duties removed
(3) Goods are, from the time they are disposed of or exported under subsection (1), no longer charged with duties levied thereon.

Custody of goods subject to seizure but not seized
103 (1) An officer may, instead of seizing any goods or conveyances that he is authorized by or pursuant to this Act to seize, leave them in the custody of the person from whom he would otherwise have seized them or any other person satisfactory to the officer.

Notice
(2) Where an officer leaves goods or a conveyance in the custody of any person pursuant to subsection (1), the officer shall give notice to the person from whom he would otherwise have seized them that he is doing so, and the goods or conveyance shall, for the purposes of this Act, be deemed to have been seized on the day the notice is given.

Conditions of custody
(3) Every person who has the custody of goods or a conveyance pursuant to subsection (1) shall hold them in safe-keeping, without charge to Her Majesty, until their forfeiture is final or a final decision is taken as to whether or not they are forfeit, and shall make them available to an officer on request, and shall not dispose of them in any manner or remove them from Canada, while he has custody of them pursuant to subsection (1), unless he is authorized to do so by an officer.

When officer to take custody
(4) An officer may at any time take custody of goods or a conveyance left in the custody of any person pursuant to subsection (1) and shall, where the forfeiture of the goods or conveyance is final,

take custody thereof.
Power to call in aid
104 An officer may call on other persons to assist him in exercising any power of search, seizure or detention that he is authorized under this Act to exercise, and any person so called on is authorized to exercise any such power.
Carrying out agreements
105 Where the Government of Canada has entered into an agreement with the government of another country pursuant to which powers, duties or functions relating to the importation of goods into Canada may be exercised or performed in that other country and powers, duties or functions relating to the importation of goods into that other country may be exercised or performed in Canada, any officer or peace officer designated for the purpose by the Minister may exercise in Canada any powers of inspection, examination, search or detention on behalf of that other country that are specified in the agreement.

Limitation of Actions or Proceedings

Limitation of action against officer or person assisting
106 (1) No action or judicial proceeding shall be commenced against an officer for anything done in the performance of his duties under this or any other Act of Parliament or a person called on to assist an officer in the performance of such duties more than three months after the time when the cause of action or the subject-matter of the proceeding arose.
Limitation of action to recover goods
(2) No action or judicial proceeding shall be commenced against the Crown, an officer or any person in possession of goods under the authority of an officer for the recovery of anything seized, detained or held in custody or safe-keeping under this Act more than three months after the later of
(a) the time when the cause of action or the subject-matter of the proceeding arose, and
(b) the final determination of the outcome of any action or proceeding taken under this Act in respect of the thing seized, detained or held in custody or safe-keeping.
Stay of action or judicial proceeding
(3) Where, in any action or judicial proceeding taken otherwise than under this Act, substantially the same facts are at issue as those that are at issue in an action or proceeding under this Act, the Minister may file a stay of proceedings with the body before whom that action or judicial proceeding is taken, and thereupon the proceedings before that body are stayed pending final determination of the outcome of the action or proceeding under this Act.

Disclosure of Information

Definitions
107 (1) The definitions in this subsection apply in this section.
customs information
(a) relates to one or more persons and is obtained by or on behalf of
(i) the Minister for the purposes of this Act or the
Customs Tariff
(ii) the Minister of National Revenue for the purposes of the collection of debts due to Her Majesty under Part V.1;
(b) is prepared from information described in paragraph (a).
official
(a) is or was employed in the service of Her Majesty in right of Canada or of a province;
(b) occupies or occupied a position of responsibility in the service of Her Majesty in right of Canada or of a province; or
(c) is or was engaged by or on behalf of Her Majesty in right of Canada or of a province.
specified person

Customs Tariff
Special Import Measures Act
Prohibition — provision or use of customs information
(2) Except as authorized under this section, no person shall
(a) knowingly provide, or allow to be provided, to any person any customs information;
(b) knowingly allow any person to have access to any customs information; or
(c) knowingly use customs information.
Authorized use of customs information by official
(3) An official may use customs information
(a) for the purposes of administering or enforcing this Act, the
Customs Tariff
Excise Act, 2001
Special Imports Measures Act
Proceeds of Crime (Money Laundering) and Terrorist Financing Act
(b) for the purposes of exercising the powers or performing the duties and functions of the Minister of Public Safety and Emergency Preparedness under the
Immigration and Refugee Protection Act
(c) for the purposes of any Act or instrument made under it, or any part of such an Act or instrument, that the Governor in Council or Parliament authorizes the Minister, the Agency, the President or an employee of the Agency to enforce, including the
Agriculture and Agri-Food Administrative Monetary Penalties Act
Canada Agricultural Products Act
Feeds Act
Fertilizers Act
Fish Inspection Act
Health of Animals Act
Meat Inspection Act
Plant Protection Act
Seeds Act
Authorized provision of information
(4) An official may provide, allow to be provided or provide access to customs information if the information
(a) will be used solely in or to prepare for criminal proceedings commenced under an Act of Parliament;
(b) will be used solely in or to prepare for any legal proceedings relating to the administration or enforcement of an international agreement relating to trade, this Act, the
Customs Tariff
Special Import Measures Act
Proceeds of Crime (Money Laundering) and Terrorist Financing Act
(i) a court of record, including a court of record in a jurisdiction outside Canada,
(ii) an international organization, or
(iii) a dispute settlement panel or an appellate body created under an international agreement relating to trade;
(c) may reasonably be regarded as necessary solely for a purpose relating to the administration or enforcement of this Act, the
Customs Tariff
Excise Act
Excise Act, 2001
Excise Tax Act
Export and Import Permits Act
Immigration and Refugee Protection Act
Special Import Measures Act

Proceeds of Crime (Money Laundering) and Terrorist Financing Act
(c.1) may reasonably be regarded as necessary solely for a purpose relating to the enforcement of the
Agriculture and Agri-Food Administrative Monetary Penalties Act
Canada Agricultural Products Act
Feeds Act
Fertilizers Act
Fish Inspection Act
Health of Animals Act
Meat Inspection Act
Plant Protection Act
Seeds Act
(c.2) may reasonably be regarded as necessary solely for a purpose relating to the administration or enforcement of Part V.1 by an official or a class of officials of the Canada Revenue Agency designated by the Minister of National Revenue;
(d) may reasonably be regarded as necessary solely for a purpose relating to the administration or enforcement of this Act, the
Excise Act
Excise Act, 2001
Export and Import Permits Act
(e) may reasonably be regarded as necessary solely for a purpose relating to the life, health or safety of an individual or to the environment in Canada or any other country;
(f) will be used solely for a purpose relating to the supervision, evaluation or discipline of a specified person by Her Majesty in right of Canada in respect of a period during which the person was employed or engaged by, or occupied a position of responsibility in the service of, Her Majesty in right of Canada to administer or enforce this Act, the
Customs Tariff
Special Import Measures Act
Proceeds of Crime (Money Laundering) and Terrorist Financing Act
(g) is reasonably regarded by the official to be information that does not directly or indirectly identify any person;
(h) is reasonably regarded by the official to be information relating to the national security or defence of Canada; or
(i) is disclosed in accordance with the
Security of Canada Information Sharing Act

Provision of information to certain persons

(5) An official may provide, allow to be provided or provide access to customs information to the following persons:
(a) a peace officer having jurisdiction to investigate an alleged offence under any Act of Parliament or of the legislature of a province subject to prosecution by indictment, the Attorney General of Canada and the Attorney General of the province in which proceedings in respect of the alleged offence may be taken, if that official believes on reasonable grounds that the information relates to the alleged offence and will be used in the investigation or prosecution of the alleged offence, solely for those purposes;
(b) a person that is otherwise legally entitled to the information by reason of an Act of Parliament, solely for the purposes for which that person is entitled to the information;
(c) an official solely for the purposes of developing, administering or enforcing an Act of Parliament or developing or implementing a policy related to an Act of Parliament if the information relates to
(i) goods, the importation, exportation or in-transit movement of which is or may be prohibited, controlled or regulated under that Act,
(ii) a person who that official has reasonable grounds to believe may have committed an offence under that Act in respect of goods imported or exported by that person, or
(iii) goods that may be evidence of an offence under that Act;

(d) an official, solely for the purpose of administering or enforcing an Act of the legislature of a province, if the information relates to goods that are subject to import, in-transit or export controls or taxation upon importation into the province under that Act;
(e) an official of a participating province, as defined in subsection 123(1) of the
Excise Tax Act
(f) an official solely for the purpose of the formulation or evaluation of fiscal or trade policy or the development of a remission order under an Act of Parliament;
(g) an official solely for the purpose of setting off, against any sum of money that may be due to or payable by Her Majesty in right of Canada, a debt due to
(i) Her Majesty in right of Canada, or
(ii) Her Majesty in right of a province on account of taxes payable to the province if an agreement exists between Canada and the province under which Canada is authorized to collect taxes on behalf of the province;
(g.1) an official of the Canada Revenue Agency solely for a purpose relating to the administration or enforcement of the
Canada Pension Plan
Employment Insurance Act
Excise Act
Excise Act, 2001
Excise Tax Act
Income Tax Act
(h) counsel, as defined in subsection 84(4) of the
Special Import Measures Act
(i) an official of the Department of Employment and Social Development solely for the purpose of administering or enforcing the
Employment Insurance Act
(j) an official of the Department of Citizenship and Immigration solely for the purpose of administering or enforcing
(i) the
Citizenship Act
Immigration and Refugee Protection Act
(ii) the law of Canada respecting passports or other travel documents;
(j.1) an official of the Canadian Food Inspection Agency for the purpose of administering or enforcing any Act referred to in section 11 of the
Canadian Food Inspection Agency Act
(k) an official of the Financial Transactions and Reports Analysis Centre of Canada solely for the purpose of administering or enforcing the
Proceeds of Crime (Money Laundering) and Terrorist Financing Act
(l) a person solely for the purpose of determining any entitlement, liability or obligation of the person under this Act or the
Customs Tariff
(l.1) any person who may receive information under section 44.03 or subsection 44.04(1) of the
Copyright Act
(l.2) any person who may receive information under section 51.05 or subsection 51.06(1) of the
Trade-marks Act
(m) any person, if the information is required to comply with a subpoena or warrant issued or an order made by a court of record in Canada;
(n) any person, if the information is required to comply with a subpoena or warrant issued or an order made by a court of record outside of Canada, solely for the purposes of criminal proceedings; and
(o) prescribed persons or classes of persons, in prescribed circumstances for prescribed purposes, solely for those purposes.

Provision of customs information by Minister
(6) The Minister may provide, allow to be provided or provide access to customs information to any person if
(a) the information may not otherwise be provided, allowed to be provided or provided access to under this section and, in the Minister's opinion, the public interest in providing the information clearly outweighs any invasion of privacy, or any material financial loss or prejudice to the competitive position of the person to whom the information relates, that could result from the provision of the information; or
(b) in the Minister's opinion, providing the information would clearly benefit the individual to whom the information relates.
Notification of Privacy Commissioner
(7) If customs information provided under subsection (6) is personal information within the meaning of section 3 of the
Privacy Act
Providing customs information to other governments
(8) Customs information may be provided by any person to an official or any other person employed by or representing the government of a foreign state, an international organization established by the governments of states, a community of states, or an institution of any such government or organization, in accordance with an international convention, agreement or other written arrangement between the Government of Canada or an institution of the Government of Canada and the government of the foreign state, the organization, the community or the institution, solely for the purposes set out in that arrangement.
Disclosure of customs information to certain persons
(9) An official may provide, allow to be provided or provide access to customs information relating to a particular person
(a) to that particular person;
(b) to a person authorized to transact business under this Act or the
Customs Tariff
(c) with the consent of that particular person, to any other person.
Evidence
(10) Despite any other Act of Parliament or other law, no official may be required, in connection with any legal proceedings, to give or produce evidence relating to any customs information.
Measures to protect customs information
(11) The person presiding at a legal proceeding relating to the supervision, evaluation or discipline of a specified person may order any measure that is necessary to ensure that customs information is not used or provided to any person for any purpose not relating to that proceeding, including
(a) holding a hearing
(b) banning the publication of the information;
(c) concealing the identity of the person to whom the information relates; and
(d) sealing the records of the proceeding.
Appeal from order to disclose customs information
(12) An order or direction that is made in the course of or in connection with any legal proceeding and that requires an official to give or produce evidence relating to customs information may, by notice served on all interested parties, be immediately appealed by the Minister or the Minister of National Revenue, as the case may be, or by the person against whom the order or direction is made
(a) to the court of appeal of the province in which the order or direction is made, in the case of an order or direction made by a court or other tribunal established under the laws of the province, whether or not that court or tribunal is exercising a jurisdiction conferred by the laws of Canada; or
(b) to the Federal Court of Appeal, in the case of an order or direction made by a court or other tribunal established under the laws of Canada.
Disposition of appeal
(13) The court to which the appeal is taken may allow the appeal and quash the order or direction

appealed from or may dismiss the appeal. The rules of practice and procedure from time to time governing appeals to the courts apply, with any modifications that the circumstances require, in respect of the appeal.
Stay
(14) An appeal stays the operation of the order or direction appealed from until judgment in the appeal is pronounced.
Regulations
(15) The Governor in Council may make regulations prescribing the circumstances in which fees may be charged for providing or providing access to customs information or making or certifying copies of information and the amount of any such fees.
R.S., 1985, c. 1 (2nd Supp.), s. 107;
1992, c. 28, s. 25;
1995, c. 41, s. 27;
2001, c. 25, ss. 61, 111, c. 41, s. 121;
2005, c. 34, s. 79, c. 38, ss. 80, 145;
2013, c. 40, s. 237;
2014, c. 32, s. 60;
2015, c. 20, s. 5.
Passenger information
107.1 (1) The Minister may, under prescribed circumstances and conditions, require any prescribed person or prescribed class of persons to provide, or to provide access to, within the prescribed time and in the prescribed manner, prescribed information about any person on board or expected to be on board a conveyance.
Disclosure
(2) Any person who is required under subsection (1) to provide, or provide access to, prescribed information shall do so despite any restriction under the
Aeronautics Act
2001, c. 25, s. 61;
2009, c. 10, s. 12;
2012, c. 31, s. 267.
108

Inquiries

Inquiry
109 (1) The Minister may, for any purpose related to the administration or enforcement of this Act, authorize any person to make an inquiry into any matter specified by the Minister.
Powers of person authorized
(2) A person authorized pursuant to subsection (1) has all of the powers of a person appointed as a commissioner under Part I of the
Inquiries Act
Travel and living expenses
(3) Reasonable travel and living expenses shall be paid to any person summoned by a person authorized under subsection (1) at the time of the service of the summons.

Penalties and Interest

Designated provisions
109.1 (1) Every person who fails to comply with any provision of an Act or a regulation designated by the regulations made under subsection (3) is liable to a penalty of not more than twenty-five thousand dollars, as the Minister may direct.
Failure to comply
(2) Every person who fails to comply with any term or condition of a licence issued under this Act or

the
Customs Tariff
Designation by regulation
(3) The Governor in Council may make regulations
(a) designating any provisions of this Act, the
Customs Tariff
Special Import Measures Act
(b) establishing short-form descriptions of the provisions designated under paragraph (a) and providing for the use of those descriptions.
1993, c. 25, s. 80;
1995, c. 41, s. 29;
1997, c. 36, s. 182;
2001, c. 25, s. 62.
109.11 Definition of
designated goods
109.2 (1) In this section,
designated goods
Customs Tariff
Contravention relating to tobacco products and designated goods
(2) Every person who
(a) removes tobacco products or designated goods or causes tobacco products or designated goods to be removed from a customs office, sufferance warehouse, bonded warehouse or duty free shop in contravention of this Act or the
Customs Tariff
(b) sells or uses tobacco products or designated goods designated as ships' stores in contravention of this Act or the
Customs Tariff
is liable to a penalty equal to double the total of the duties that would be payable on like tobacco products or designated goods released in like condition at the rates of duties applicable to like tobacco products or designated goods at the time the penalty is assessed, or to such lesser amount as the Minister may direct.
1993, c. 25, s. 80;
1995, c. 41, s. 29;
1997, c. 36, s. 184.
Assessment
109.3 (1) A penalty to which a person is liable under section 109.1 or 109.2 may be assessed by an officer and, if an assessment is made, an officer shall serve on the person a written notice of that assessment by sending it by registered or certified mail or delivering it to the person.
Limitation on assessment
(2) A person shall not be assessed penalties under both sections 109.1 and 109.2 in respect of the same contravention of this Act, the
Customs Tariff
Special Import Measures Act
Penalty in addition to other sanction
(3) An assessment under subsection (1) may be made in addition to a seizure under this Act or a demand for payment under section 124, in respect of the same contravention of this Act or the regulations.
Sufficiency of short-form description
(4) The use on a notice of assessment of a short-form description established under paragraph 109.1(3)(b) or of a description that deviates from that description without affecting its substance is sufficient for all purposes to describe the contravention.
1993, c. 25, s. 80;

1995, c. 41, s. 30;
2001, c. 25, s. 63.

When penalty becomes payable
109.4 A penalty assessed against a person under section 109.3 shall become payable on the day the notice of assessment of the penalty is served on the person.
1993, c. 25, s. 80.

Interest on penalties
109.5 (1) Subject to subsection (2), a person on whom a notice of assessment of a penalty has been served under section 109.3 shall pay, in addition to the penalty, interest at the prescribed rate for the period beginning on the day after the notice was served on the person and ending on the day the penalty has been paid in full, calculated on the outstanding balance of the penalty.

Exception
(2) Interest is not payable if the penalty is paid in full by the person within thirty days after the date of the notice of assessment.
1993, c. 25, s. 80;
2001, c. 25, s. 64.

Seizures

Seizure of goods or conveyances
110 (1) An officer may, where he believes on reasonable grounds that this Act or the regulations have been contravened in respect of goods, seize as forfeit
(a) the goods; or
(b) any conveyance that the officer believes on reasonable grounds was made use of in respect of the goods, whether at or after the time of the contravention.

Seizure of conveyances
(2) An officer may, where he believes on reasonable grounds that this Act or the regulations have been contravened in respect of a conveyance or in respect of persons transported by a conveyance, seize as forfeit the conveyance.

Seizure of evidence
(3) An officer may, where he believes on reasonable grounds that this Act or the regulations have been contravened, seize anything that he believes on reasonable grounds will afford evidence in respect of the contravention.

Notice of seizure
(4) An officer who seizes goods or a conveyance as forfeit under subsection (1) or (2) shall take such measures as are reasonable in the circumstances to give notice of the seizure to any person who the officer believes on reasonable grounds is entitled to make an application under section 138 in respect of the goods or conveyance.

Information for search warrant
111 (1) A justice of the peace who is satisfied by information on oath in the form set out as Form 1 in Part XXVIII of the
Criminal Code
(a) any goods or conveyance in respect of which this Act or the regulations have been contravened or are suspected of having been contravened,
(b) any conveyance that has been made use of in respect of such goods, whether at or after the time of the contravention, or
(c) anything that there are reasonable grounds to believe will afford evidence in respect of a contravention of this Act or the regulations,
may at any time issue a warrant under his hand authorizing an officer to search the building, receptacle or place for any such thing and to seize it.

Execution in another territorial jurisdiction
(2) A justice of the peace may, where a building, receptacle or place referred to in subsection (1) is in

a territorial division other than that in which the justice of the peace has jurisdiction, issue his warrant in a form similar to the form referred to in subsection (1), modified according to the circumstances, and the warrant may be executed in the other territorial division after it has been endorsed, in the manner set out in Form 28 of Part XXVIII of the
Criminal Code

Seizure of things not specified

(3) An officer who executes a warrant issued under subsection (1) may seize, in addition to the things mentioned in the warrant,

(a) any goods or conveyance in respect of which the officer believes on reasonable grounds that this Act or the regulations have been contravened;

(b) any conveyance that the officer believes on reasonable grounds was made use of in respect of such goods, whether at or after the time of the contravention; or

(c) anything that the officer believes on reasonable grounds will afford evidence in respect of a contravention of this Act or the regulations.

Execution of search warrant

(4) A warrant issued under subsection (1) shall be executed by day, unless the justice of the peace, by the warrant, authorizes execution of it by night.

Form of search warrant

(5) A warrant issued under subsection (1) may be in the form set out as Form 5 in Part XXVIII of the Criminal Code

Where warrant not necessary

(6) An officer may exercise any of the powers referred to in subsection (1) without a warrant if the conditions for obtaining the warrant exist but by reason of exigent circumstances it would not be practical to obtain the warrant.

Exigent circumstances

(7) For the purposes of subsection (6), exigent circumstances include circumstances in which the delay necessary to obtain a warrant under subsection (1) would result in danger to human life or safety or the loss or destruction of anything liable to seizure.

R.S., 1985, c. 1 (2nd Supp.), s. 111;

1992, c. 1, s. 143(E).

Powers of entry

112 For the purpose of exercising his authority under section 111, an officer may, with such assistance as he deems necessary, break open any door, window, lock, fastener, floor, wall, ceiling, compartment, plumbing fixture, box, container or any other thing.

Limitation for seizures and ascertained forfeitures

113 No seizure may be made under this Act or notice sent under section 124 more than six years after the contravention or use in respect of which such seizure is made or notice is sent.

Custody of things seized

114 (1) Anything that is seized under this Act shall forthwith be placed in the custody of an officer.

Report where evidence seized

(2) Where an officer seizes anything as evidence under this Act, the officer shall forthwith report the circumstances of the case to the President.

Return of evidence

(3) Anything that is seized under this Act as evidence alone shall be returned forthwith on completion of all proceedings in which the thing seized may be required.

R.S., 1985, c. 1 (2nd Supp.), s. 114;

1999, c. 17, s. 127;

2005, c. 38, s. 85.

Copies of records

115 (1) If any record is examined or seized under this Act, the Minister, or the officer by whom it is examined or seized, may make or cause to be made one or more copies of it, and a copy purporting to be certified by the Minister or a person authorized by the Minister is admissible in evidence and

has the same probative force as the original would have if it had been proved in the ordinary way.
Detention of records seized
(2) No record that has been seized as evidence under this Act shall be detained for a period of more than three months unless, before the expiration of that period,
(a) the person from whom it was seized agrees to its further detention for a specified period;
(b) a justice of the peace is satisfied on application that, having regard to the circumstances, its further detention for a specified period is warranted and he or she so orders; or
(c) judicial proceedings are instituted in which the seized record may be required.
R.S., 1985, c. 1 (2nd Supp.), s. 115;
2001, c. 25, s. 65.
Goods stopped or taken by peace officer
116 Where a peace officer detains or seizes anything that he suspects is subject to seizure under this Act, he shall forthwith notify an officer thereof and describe the thing detained or seized to the officer.

Return of Goods Seized

Return of goods seized
117 (1) An officer may, subject to this or any other Act of Parliament, return any goods that have been seized under this Act to the person from whom they were seized or to any person authorized by the person from whom they were seized on receipt of
(a) an amount of money of a value equal to
(i) the aggregate of the value for duty of the goods and the amount of duties levied thereon, if any, calculated at the rates applicable thereto
(A) at the time of seizure, if the goods have not been accounted for under subsection 32(1), (2) or (5) or if duties or additional duties have become due on the goods under paragraph 32.2(2)(b) in circumstances to which subsection 32.2(6) applies, or
(B) at the time the goods were accounted for under subsection 32(1), (2) or (5), in any other case, or
(ii) such lesser amount as the Minister may direct; or
(b) where the Minister so authorizes, security satisfactory to the Minister.
No return of certain goods
(2) Despite subsection (1), if spirits, wine, specially denatured alcohol, restricted formulations, raw leaf tobacco, excise stamps or tobacco products are seized under this Act, they shall not be returned to the person from whom they were seized or any other person unless they were seized in error.
R.S., 1985, c. 1 (2nd Supp.), s. 117;
1995, c. 41, s. 31;
1997, c. 36, s. 185;
2002, c. 22, s. 338;
2007, c. 18, s. 137;
2010, c. 12, s. 50.
Return of conveyance seized
118 An officer may, subject to this or any other Act of Parliament, return any conveyance that has been seized under this Act to the person from whom it was seized or to any person authorized by the person from whom it was seized on receipt of
(a) an amount of money of a value equal to
(i) the value of the conveyance at the time of seizure, as determined by the Minister, or
(ii) such lesser amount as the Minister may direct; or
(b) where the Minister so authorizes, security satisfactory to the Minister.
Return of animals or perishable goods seized
119 (1) An officer shall, subject to this or any other Act of Parliament, return any animals or perishable goods that have been seized under this Act and have not been sold under subsection (2) to the person from whom they were seized or to any person authorized by the person from whom they

were seized at the request of such person and on receipt of
(a) an amount of money of a value equal to
(i) the aggregate of the value for duty of the animals or perishable goods and the amount of duties levied thereon, if any, calculated at the rates applicable thereto,
(A) at the time of seizure, if the animals or perishable goods have not been accounted for under subsection 32(1), (2) or (5) or if duties or additional duties have become due on the goods under paragraph 32.2(2)(b) in circumstances to which subsection 32.2(6) applies, or
(B) at the time the animals or perishable goods were accounted for under subsection 32(1), (2) or (5), in any other case, or
(ii) such lesser amount as the Minister may direct; or
(b) where the Minister so authorizes, security satisfactory to the Minister.

Sale of seized goods

(2) An officer may sell any animals or perishable goods that have been seized under this Act, in order to avoid the expense of keeping them or to avoid their deterioration, at any time after giving the person from whom they were seized or the owner thereof a reasonable opportunity to obtain the animals or perishable goods under subsection (1), and the proceeds of the sale shall be held as forfeit in lieu of the thing sold.

R.S., 1985, c. 1 (2nd Supp.), s. 119;
1995, c. 41, s. 32;
1997, c. 36, s. 186.

Dealing with goods seized

119.1 (1) Where any goods are seized under this Act, the Minister may authorize an officer to sell, destroy or otherwise deal with the goods.

Excise stamps not to be sold

(1.01) Despite subsection (1), the Minister shall not authorize an officer to sell excise stamps that have been seized under this Act.

Restriction

(1.1) Subject to the regulations, the sale under subsection (1) of
(a) spirits or specially denatured alcohol may only be to a spirits licensee;
(b) wine may only be to a wine licensee;
(c) raw leaf tobacco or a tobacco product may only be to a tobacco licensee; and
(d) a restricted formulation may only be to a licensed user.

Proceeds of sale

(2) The Minister shall hold the proceeds from the sale of any goods under subsection (1) as forfeit in lieu of the goods sold.

Payment of compensation

(3) Where a person would be entitled to the return of goods if they were available to be returned, but it is not possible to return them, the person shall be paid
(a) where the goods were sold, the proceeds from the sale; and
(b) in any other case, the value of the goods.

1994, c. 37, s. 9;
2002, c. 22, s. 339;
2007, c. 18, s. 138;
2010, c. 12, s. 51.

Value substituted for value for duty

120 For the purpose of calculating the amount of money referred to in paragraph 117(a) or 119(1)(a), where the value for duty of goods cannot be ascertained, the value of the goods at the time of seizure, as determined by the Minister, may be substituted for the value for duty thereof.

Goods no longer forfeit

121 Goods or conveyances in respect of which money or security is received under section 117, 118 or 119 shall cease to be forfeit from the time the money or security is received and the money or security shall be held as forfeit in lieu thereof.

Forfeitures

General

Forfeitures accrue automatically from time of contravention
122 Subject to the reviews and appeals established by this Act, any goods or conveyances that are seized as forfeit under this Act within the time period set out in section 113 are forfeit
(a) from the time of the contravention of this Act or the regulations in respect of which the goods or conveyances were seized, or
(b) in the case of a conveyance made use of in respect of goods in respect of which this Act or the regulations have been contravened, from the time of such use,
and no act or proceeding subsequent to the contravention or use is necessary to effect the forfeiture of such goods or conveyances.
Review of forfeiture
123 The forfeiture of goods or conveyances seized under this Act or any money or security held as forfeit in lieu of such goods or conveyances is final and not subject to review or to be restrained, prohibited, removed, set aside or otherwise dealt with except to the extent and in the manner provided by sections 127.1 and 129.
R.S., 1985, c. 1 (2nd Supp.), s. 123;
2001, c. 25, s. 66.

Ascertained Forfeiture

Ascertained forfeitures
124 (1) Where an officer believes on reasonable grounds that a person has contravened any of the provisions of this Act or the regulations in respect of any goods or conveyance, the officer may, if the goods or conveyance is not found or if the seizure thereof would be impractical, serve a written notice on that person demanding payment of
(a) an amount of money determined under subsection (2) or (3), as the case may be; or
(b) such lesser amount as the Minister may direct.
Determination of amount of payment in respect of goods
(2) For the purpose of paragraph (1)(a), an officer may demand payment in respect of goods of an amount of money of a value equal to the aggregate of the value for duty of the goods and the amount of duties levied thereon, if any, calculated at the rates applicable thereto
(a) at the time the notice is served, if the goods have not been accounted for under subsection 32(1), (2) or (5) or if duties or additional duties have become due on the goods under paragraph 32.2(2)(b) in circumstances to which subsection 32.2(6) applies; or
(b) at the time the goods were accounted for under subsection 32(1), (2) or (5), in any other case.
Determination of amount of payment in respect of conveyances
(3) For the purpose of paragraph (1)(a), an officer may demand payment in respect of a conveyance of an amount of money of a value equal to the value of the conveyance at the time the notice is served, as determined by the Minister.
Value substituted for value for duty
(4) For the purpose of calculating the amount of money referred to in subsection (2), where the value for duty of goods cannot be ascertained, the value of the goods at the time the notice is served under subsection (1), as determined by the Minister, may be substituted for the value for duty thereof.
Value of exported goods
(4.1) Sections 117 and 119 and subsection (2) apply to a contravention of this Act or the regulations in respect of goods that have been or are about to be exported, except that the references to "value for duty of the goods" in those provisions are to be read as references to "value of the goods".
Value of goods

(4.2) For the purposes of subsection (4.1), the expression value of the goods
Value of goods set by Minister
(4.3) If the value of the goods cannot be determined under subsection (4.2), the Minister may determine that value.
Service of notice
(5) Service of the notice referred to in subsection (1) is sufficient if it is sent by registered mail addressed to the person on whom it is to be served at his latest known address.
Interest
(6) A person on whom a notice of ascertained forfeiture has been served shall pay, in addition to the amount set out in the notice, interest at the prescribed rate for the period beginning on the day after the notice was served and ending on the day the amount is paid in full, calculated on the outstanding balance. However, interest is not payable if the amount is paid in full within thirty days after the date of the notice.
R.S., 1985, c. 1 (2nd Supp.), s. 124;
1995, c. 41, s. 33;
1997, c. 36, s. 187;
2001, c. 25, s. 67.
Seizure cancels notice
125 The seizure under this Act of anything in respect of which a notice is served under section 124, except as evidence alone, constitutes a cancellation of the notice where the notice and the seizure are in respect of the same contravention.
Limitation respecting seizure
126 Nothing in respect of which a notice is served under section 124 is, from the time the amount demanded in the notice is paid or from the time a decision of the Minister under section 131 is requested in respect of the amount demanded, subject to seizure under this Act in respect of the same contravention except as evidence alone.

Review of Seizure, Ascertained Forfeiture or Penalty Assessment

No review or appeal
126.1 Sections 127 to 133 do not apply to a contravention of subsection 40(3) of this Act by a person referred to in paragraph (c) of that subsection, or to a contravention of section 32.2 of this Act in circumstances to which subsection 32.2(6) of this Act applies, or to a contravention of subsection 95(1), 118(1) or (2), 121(1) or 122(1) of the
Customs Tariff
1995, c. 41, s. 34;
1997, c. 36, s. 188.
Review of ascertained forfeiture or penalty assessment
127 The debt due to Her Majesty as a result of a notice served under section 109.3 or a demand under section 124 is final and not subject to review or to be restrained, prohibited, removed, set aside or otherwise dealt with except to the extent and in the manner provided by sections 127.1 and 129.
R.S., 1985, c. 1 (2nd Supp.), s. 127;
1993, c. 25, s. 81;
2001, c. 25, s. 68.
Corrective measures
127.1 (1) The Minister, or any officer designated by the President for the purposes of this section, may cancel a seizure made under section 110, cancel or reduce a penalty assessed under section 109.3 or an amount demanded under section 124 or refund an amount received under any of sections 117 to 119 within 90 days after the seizure, assessment or demand, if
(a) the Minister is satisfied that there was no contravention; or
(b) there was a contravention but the Minister considers that there was an error with respect to the

amount assessed, collected, demanded or taken as security and that the amount should be reduced.
Interest
(2) If an amount is returned to a person under paragraph (1)(a), the person shall be given interest on that amount at the prescribed rate for the period beginning on the day after the amount was originally paid by that person and ending on the day it was returned.
2001, c. 25, s. 68;
2005, c. 38, s. 81;
2009, c. 10, s. 13(F);
2014, c. 20, s. 172.
Report to President
128 Where goods or a conveyance has been seized under this Act, or a notice has been served under section 109.3 or 124, the officer who seized the goods or conveyance or served the notice or caused it to be served shall forthwith report the circumstances of the case to the President.
R.S., 1985, c. 1 (2nd Supp.), s. 128;
1993, c. 25, s. 81;
1999, c. 17, s. 127;
2005, c. 38, s. 85.
Request for Minister's decision
129 (1) The following persons may, within 90 days after the date of a seizure or the service of a notice, request a decision of the Minister under section 131 by giving notice to the Minister in writing or by any other means that is satisfactory to the Minister:
(a) any person from whom goods or a conveyance is seized under this Act;
(b) any person who owns goods or a conveyance that is seized under this Act;
(c) any person from whom money or security is received pursuant to section 117, 118 or 119 in respect of goods or a conveyance seized under this Act; or
(d) any person on whom a notice is served under section 109.3 or 124.
Burden of proof
(2) The burden of proof that notice was given under subsection (1) lies on the person claiming to have given the notice.
R.S., 1985, c. 1 (2nd Supp.), s. 129;
1993, c. 25, s. 82;
2001, c. 25, s. 69;
2014, c. 20, s. 173.
Extension of time by Minister
129.1 (1) If no request for a decision of the Minister is made under section 129 within the time provided in that section, a person may apply in writing to the Minister for an extension of the time for making the request and the Minister may grant the application.
Reasons
(2) An application must set out the reasons why the request was not made on time.
Burden of proof of application
(3) The burden of proof that an application has been made under subsection (1) lies on the person claiming to have made it.
Notice of decision
(4) The Minister must, without delay after making a decision in respect of an application, notify the applicant in writing of the decision.
Conditions for granting application
(5) The application may not be granted unless
(a) it is made within one year after the expiration of the time provided in section 129; and
(b) the applicant demonstrates that
(i) within the time provided in section 129, the applicant was unable to request a decision or to instruct another person to request a decision on the applicant's behalf or the applicant had a
(ii) it would be just and equitable to grant the application, and

(iii) the application was made as soon as circumstances permitted.
2001, c. 25, s. 70.

Extension of time by Federal Court

129.2 (1) A person may apply to the Federal Court to have their application under section 129.1 granted if
(a) the Minister dismisses that application; or
(b) ninety days have expired after the application was made and the Minister has not notified the person of a decision made in respect of it.
If paragraph (a) applies, the application under this subsection must be made within ninety days after the application is dismissed.

Application process

(2) The application must be made by filing a copy of the application made under section 129.1, and any notice given in respect of it, with the Minister and the Administrator of the Court.

Powers of the Court

(3) The Court may grant or dismiss the application and, if it grants the application, may impose any terms that it considers just or order that the request under section 129 be deemed to have been made on the date the order was made.

Conditions for granting application

(4) The application may not be granted unless
(a) the application under subsection 129.1(1) was made within one year after the expiration of the time provided in section 129; and
(b) the person making the application demonstrates that
(i) within the time provided in section 129 for making a request for a decision of the Minister, the person was unable to act or to instruct another person to act in the person's name or had a
(ii) it would be just and equitable to grant the application, and
(iii) the application was made as soon as circumstances permitted.
2001, c. 25, s. 70.

Notice of reasons for action

130 (1) Where a decision of the Minister under section 131 is requested under section 129, the President shall forthwith serve on the person who requested the decision written notice of the reasons for the seizure, or for the notice served under section 109.3 or 124, in respect of which the decision is requested.

Evidence

(2) The person on whom a notice is served under subsection (1) may, within thirty days after the notice is served, furnish such evidence in the matter as he desires to furnish.

Evidence

(3) Evidence may be given under subsection (2) by affidavit made before any person authorized by an Act of Parliament or of the legislature of a province to administer oaths or take affidavits.
R.S., 1985, c. 1 (2nd Supp.), s. 130;
1993, c. 25, s. 83;
1999, c. 17, s. 127;
2001, c. 25, s. 71;
2005, c. 38, s. 85.

Decision of the Minister

131 (1) After the expiration of the thirty days referred to in subsection 130(2), the Minister shall, as soon as is reasonably possible having regard to the circumstances, consider and weigh the circumstances of the case and decide
(a) in the case of goods or a conveyance seized or with respect to which a notice was served under section 124 on the ground that this Act or the regulations were contravened in respect of the goods or the conveyance, whether the Act or the regulations were so contravened;
(b) in the case of a conveyance seized or in respect of which a notice was served under section 124 on the ground that it was made use of in respect of goods in respect of which this Act or the

regulations were contravened, whether the conveyance was made use of in that way and whether the Act or the regulations were so contravened; or

(c) in the case of a penalty assessed under section 109.3 against a person for failure to comply with subsection 109.1(1) or (2) or a provision that is designated under subsection 109.1(3), whether the person so failed to comply.

(d) Exception

(1.1) A person on whom a notice is served under section 130 may notify the Minister, in writing, that the person will not be furnishing evidence under that section and authorize the Minister to make a decision without delay in the matter.

Notice of decision

(2) The Minister shall, forthwith on making a decision under subsection (1), serve on the person who requested the decision a detailed written notice of the decision.

Judicial review

(3) The Minister's decision under subsection (1) is not subject to review or to be restrained, prohibited, removed, set aside or otherwise dealt with except to the extent and in the manner provided by subsection 135(1).

R.S., 1985, c. 1 (2nd Supp.), s. 131;

1993, c. 25, s. 84;

2001, c. 25, s. 72.

Where there is no contravention

132 (1) Subject to this or any other Act of Parliament,

(a) where the Minister decides, under paragraph 131(1)(a) or (b), that there has been no contravention of this Act or the regulations in respect of the goods or conveyance referred to in that paragraph, or, under paragraph 131(1)(b), that the conveyance referred to in that paragraph was not used in the manner described in that paragraph, the Minister shall forthwith authorize the removal from custody of the goods or conveyance or the return of any money or security taken in respect of the goods or conveyance; and

(b) where, as a result of a decision made by the Minister under paragraph 131(1)(c), the Minister decides that a penalty that was assessed under section 109.3 is not justified by the facts or the law, the Minister shall forthwith cancel the assessment of the penalty and authorize the return of any money paid on account of the penalty and any interest that was paid under section 109.5 in respect of the penalty.

Interest on money returned

(2) Where any money is authorized under subsection (1) to be returned to any person, there shall be paid to that person, in addition to the money returned, interest on the money at the prescribed rate for the period beginning on the day after the day the money was paid and ending on the day the money is returned.

(3) R.S., 1985, c. 1 (2nd Supp.), s. 132;

1992, c. 28, s. 26;

1993, c. 25, s. 85;

2001, c. 25, s. 73.

Where there is contravention

133 (1) Where the Minister decides, under paragraph 131(1)(a) or (b), that there has been a contravention of this Act or the regulations in respect of the goods or conveyance referred to in that paragraph, and, in the case of a conveyance referred to in paragraph 131(1)(b), that it was used in the manner described in that paragraph, the Minister may, subject to such terms and conditions as the Minister may determine,

(a) return the goods or conveyance on receipt of an amount of money of a value equal to an amount determined under subsection (2) or (3), as the case may be;

(b) remit any portion of any money or security taken; and

(c) where the Minister considers that insufficient money or security was taken or where no money or security was received, demand such amount of money as he considers sufficient, not exceeding an

amount determined under subsection (4) or (5), as the case may be.
Powers of Minister
(1.1) If the Minister decides under paragraph 131(1)(c) that the person failed to comply, the Minister may, subject to any terms and conditions that the Minister may determine,
(a) remit any portion of the penalty assessed under section 109.3; or
(b) demand that an additional amount be paid.
If an additional amount is demanded, the total of the amount assessed and the additional amount may not exceed the maximum penalty that could be assessed under section 109.3.
Return of goods under paragraph (1)(a)
(2) Goods may be returned under paragraph (1)(a) on receipt of an amount of money of a value equal to
(a) the aggregate of the value for duty of the goods and the amount of duties levied thereon, if any, calculated at the rates applicable thereto
(i) at the time of seizure, if the goods have not been accounted for under subsection 32(1), (2) or (5) or if duties or additional duties have become due on the goods under paragraph 32.2(2)(b) in circumstances to which subsection 32.2(6) applies, or
(ii) at the time the goods were accounted for under subsection 32(1), (2) or (5), in any other case; or
(b) such lesser amount as the Minister may direct.
Return of a conveyance under paragraph (1)(a)
(3) A conveyance may be returned under paragraph (1)(a) on receipt of an amount of money of a value equal to
(a) the value of the conveyance at the time of seizure, as determined by the Minister; or
(b) such lesser amount as the Minister may direct.
Amount demanded in respect of goods under paragraph (1)(c)
(4) The amount of money that the Minister may demand under paragraph (1)(c) in respect of goods shall not exceed an amount equal to the aggregate of the value for duty of the goods and the amount of duties levied thereon, if any, calculated at the rates applicable thereto,
(a) at the time of seizure or of service of the notice under section 124, if the goods have not been accounted for under subsection 32(1), (2) or (5) or if duties or additional duties have become due on the goods under paragraph 32.2(2)(b) in circumstances to which subsection 32.2(6) applies; or
(b) at the time the goods were accounted for under subsection 32(1), (2) or (5), in any other case.
Amount demanded in respect of conveyance under paragraph (1)(c)
(5) The amount of money that the Minister may demand under paragraph (1)(c) in respect of a conveyance shall not exceed an amount equal to the value of the conveyance at the time of seizure or of service of the notice under section 124, as determined by the Minister.
Value substituted for value for duty
(6) For the purpose of calculating the amount of money referred to in subsection (2) or (4), where the value for duty of goods cannot be ascertained, the value of the goods at the time of seizure or of service of the notice under section 124, as determined by the Minister, may be substituted for the value for duty thereof.
Interest
(7) If an amount of money is demanded under paragraph (1)(c) or (1.1)(b), the person to whom the demand is made shall pay the amount demanded together with interest at the prescribed rate for the period beginning on the day after the notice is served under subsection 131(2) and ending on the day the amount has been paid in full, calculated on the outstanding balance of the amount. However, interest is not payable if the amount demanded is paid in full within thirty days after the notice is served.
(8) R.S., 1985, c. 1 (2nd Supp.), s. 133;
1992, c. 28, s. 27;
1993, c. 25, s. 86;
1995, c. 41, s. 35;
1997, c. 36, s. 189;

2001, c. 25, s. 74.
134 Federal Court
135 (1) A person who requests a decision of the Minister under section 131 may, within ninety days after being notified of the decision, appeal the decision by way of an action in the Federal Court in which that person is the plaintiff and the Minister is the defendant.
Ordinary action
(2) The
Federal Courts Act
R.S., 1985, c. 1 (2nd Supp.), s. 135;
1990, c. 8, s. 49;
2002, c. 8, s. 134.
Restoration of goods pending appeal
136 Where an appeal is taken by the Crown from any judgment that orders the Crown to give or return anything that has been seized under this Act to any person, the execution of the judgment shall not be suspended if the person to whom the goods are ordered given or returned gives such security to the Crown as the court that rendered the judgment, or a judge thereof, considers sufficient to ensure delivery of the goods or the full value thereof to the Crown if the judgment so appealed is reversed.
Service of notices
137 The service of the President's notice under section 130 or the notice of the Minister's decision under section 131 is sufficient if it is sent by registered mail addressed to the person on whom it is to be served at his latest known address.
R.S., 1985, c. 1 (2nd Supp.), s. 137;
1999, c. 17, s. 127;
2005, c. 38, s. 85.

Third Party Claims

Third party claims
138 (1) If goods or a conveyance is seized as forfeit under this Act or if a conveyance is detained under subsection 97.25(2), any person, other than the person in whose possession it was when seized or detained, who claims an interest in it as owner, mortgagee, hypothecary creditor, lien-holder or holder of any like interest may, within ninety days after the seizure or detention, apply for a decision by the Minister under section 139.
Application procedure
(2) A person may apply for a decision by giving notice to the Minister in writing or by any other means that is satisfactory to the Minister.
Burden of proof of application
(3) The burden of proof that an application has been made under subsection (1) lies on the person claiming to have made it.
Provision of evidence
(4) A person who applies under subsection (1) must provide evidence that relates to their interest in the seized or detained goods or conveyance and any other evidence requested by the Minister in respect of that interest.
Manner of giving evidence
(5) Evidence may be given under subsection (4) by affidavit made before any person authorized by an Act of Parliament or of the legislature of a province to administer oaths or take affidavits.
Late applications
(6) The Minister may accept an application made within one year after the expiration of the ninety days referred to in subsection (1) by a person who has not claimed an interest in the seized or detained goods or conveyance within those ninety days.
Conditions for late applications

(7) When making an application under subsection (6), the person must demonstrate to the Minister that
(a) within the time provided in subsection (1) for making an application the person
(i) was unable to act or to instruct another person to act in the person's name, or
(ii) had a
(b) it would be just and equitable to grant the application; and
(c) the application was made as soon as circumstances permitted.
R.S., 1985, c. 1 (2nd Supp.), s. 138;
1992, c. 1, s. 62, c. 51, s. 45;
1998, c. 30, s. 14;
1999, c. 3, s. 60, c. 17, s. 127;
2001, c. 25, s. 75;
2014, c. 20, s. 174;
2015, c. 3, s. 62(F).

Decision of Minister
139 The Minister must decide an application made under section 138 without delay and, if the Minister is satisfied that the following conditions are met, must make a determination that the applicant's interest in the goods or conveyance is not affected by the seizure or detention and as to the nature and extent of the applicant's interest at the time of the contravention or use:
(a) the applicant acquired the interest in good faith before the contravention or use;
(b) the applicant is innocent of any complicity or collusion in the contravention or use; and
(c) the applicant exercised all reasonable care in respect of any person permitted to obtain possession of the goods or conveyance in order to satisfy the applicant that it was not likely to be used in a contravention or, if the applicant is a mortgagee, hypothecary creditor or lien-holder, the applicant exercised that care in relation to the mortgagor, hypothecary debtor or lien-giver.
R.S., 1985, c. 1 (2nd Supp.), s. 139;
2001, c. 25, s. 75.

Order
139.1 (1) A person who makes an application under section 138 may, within ninety days after being notified of the decision, apply for an order under this section by giving notice in writing to the court.

Meaning of
court
(2) In this section,
court
(a) in the Province of Ontario, the Superior Court of Justice;
(b) in the Province of Quebec, the Superior Court;
(c) in the Provinces of Nova Scotia, British Columbia and Prince Edward Island, Yukon and the Northwest Territories, the Supreme Court;
(d) in the Provinces of New Brunswick, Manitoba, Saskatchewan and Alberta, the Court of Queen's Bench;
(e) in the Province of Newfoundland and Labrador, the Trial Division of the Supreme Court; and
(f) in Nunavut, the Nunavut Court of Justice.

Date of hearing
(3) A judge of the court must fix a day, not less than thirty days after the application has been made, for the hearing of the application.

Notice to Minister
(4) The applicant, no later than fifteen days before the day fixed for the hearing, must serve notice of the application and of the hearing on the Minister, or an officer designated by the Minister for the purposes of this section.

Service by registered mail
(5) Service of the notice is sufficient if it is sent by registered mail addressed to the Minister.

Order

(6) The applicant is entitled to an order declaring that the applicant's interest is not affected by the seizure or detention and declaring the nature and extent of the applicant's interest at the time of the contravention or use if, on the hearing of the application, the court is satisfied that the applicant
(a) acquired the interest in good faith prior to the contravention or use;
(b) is innocent of any complicity or collusion in the contravention or use; and
(c) exercised all reasonable care in respect of any person permitted to obtain possession of the goods or conveyance in order to satisfy the applicant that it was not likely to be used in a contravention or, if the applicant is a mortgagee, hypothecary creditor or lien-holder, that the applicant exercised that care in relation to the mortgagor, hypothecary debtor or lien-giver.
2001, c. 25, s. 75;
2002, c. 7, s. 272;
2009, c. 10, s. 14(F);
2015, c. 3, s. 63.

Appeal
140 (1) A person who makes an application under section 139.1 or the Crown may appeal to the court of appeal from an order made under that section and the appeal shall be asserted, heard and decided according to the ordinary procedure governing appeals to the court of appeal from orders or judgments of a court.

Definition of
court of appeal
(2) In this section,
court of appeal
Criminal Code
R.S., 1985, c. 1 (2nd Supp.), s. 140;
2001, c. 25, s. 76.

Goods or conveyance given to applicant
141 (1) The President, on application by a person whose interest in a conveyance detained under subsection 97.25(2) or in goods or a conveyance seized as forfeit under this Act has been determined under section 139 or ordered under section 139.1 or 140 to be unaffected by the seizure or detention, shall direct that
(a) in the case of goods or a conveyance the forfeiture of which has become final, the goods or conveyance, as the case may be, be given to the applicant; and
(b) in the case of a conveyance detained under subsection 97.25(2), the conveyance be given to the applicant.

Amount paid if goods or conveyance sold
(1.1) If goods or a conveyance that is to be given to the applicant has been sold or disposed of, an amount calculated on the basis of the interest of the applicant in the goods or conveyance at the time of the contravention or use, as determined under section 139 or ordered under section 139.1 or 140, shall be paid to the applicant.

Limit on amount paid
(2) The total amount paid under subsection (1.1) in respect of goods or a conveyance shall, if the goods or conveyance was sold or otherwise disposed of under this Act, not exceed the proceeds of the sale or disposition, if any, less any costs incurred by Her Majesty in respect of the goods or conveyance, and, if there are no proceeds of disposition, no payment shall be made pursuant to subsection (1.1).
R.S., 1985, c. 1 (2nd Supp.), s. 141;
1999, c. 17, s. 127;
2001, c. 25, s. 77;
2005, c. 38, s. 85.

Disposal of Things Abandoned or Forfeit

Disposal of things abandoned or forfeit
142 (1) Unless the thing is spirits, specially denatured alcohol, a restricted formulation, wine, raw leaf tobacco, an excise stamp or a tobacco product, anything that has been abandoned to Her Majesty in right of Canada under this Act and anything the forfeiture of which is final under this Act shall
(a) where the Minister deems it appropriate, be exported;
(b) where the importation thereof is prohibited, or where the Minister considers the thing to be unsuitable for sale or of insufficient value to justify a sale, be disposed of in such manner, otherwise than by sale, as the Minister may direct; and
(c) in any other case, be sold by public auction or public tender or by the Minister of Public Works and Government Services pursuant to the
Surplus Crown Assets Act
Duties removed
(2) Any goods that are disposed of pursuant to subsection (1) are, from the time of disposal, no longer charged with duties.
R.S., 1985, c. 1 (2nd Supp.), s. 142;
1996, c. 16, s. 60;
2002, c. 22, s. 340;
2007, c. 18, s. 139;
2010, c. 12, s. 52.
Dealing with abandoned or forfeited alcohol, etc.
142.1 (1) If spirits, specially denatured alcohol, a restricted formulation, wine, raw leaf tobacco or a tobacco product is abandoned or finally forfeited under this Act, the Minister may sell, destroy or otherwise deal with it.
Dealing with abandoned or forfeited excise stamps
(1.1) If an excise stamp is abandoned or finally forfeited under this Act, the Minister may destroy or otherwise deal with it.
Restriction
(2) Subject to the regulations, the sale under subsection (1) of
(a) spirits or specially denatured alcohol may only be to a spirits licensee;
(b) wine may only be to a wine licensee;
(c) raw leaf tobacco or a tobacco product may only be to a tobacco licensee; and
(d) a restricted formulation may only be to a licensed user.
2002, c. 22, s. 341;
2007, c. 18, s. 140;
2010, c. 12, s. 53.
143 to 147

Collection of Duties on Mail

Definition
147.1 (1) In this section,
Corporation
Application
(2) Subsections (3) to (13) apply to mail except as may be provided in regulations made under paragraph (14)(e).
Collection agreement
(3) The Minister and the Corporation may enter into an agreement in writing whereby the Minister authorizes the Corporation to collect, as agent of the Minister, duties in respect of mail and the Corporation agrees to collect the duties as agent of the Minister.
Terms and conditions
(4) An agreement made under subsection (3) relating to the collection of duties in respect of mail may provide for the terms and conditions under which and the period during which the Corporation is authorized to collect the duties and for other matters in relation to the administration of this Act in

respect of such mail.
Authorization by Corporation
(5) The Corporation may authorize in writing any person to collect, as its agent, duties under terms and conditions consistent with those provided for in the agreement made under subsection (3) and during a period not exceeding the period provided for in that agreement.
Liability to pay duties
(6) Where the Corporation has entered into an agreement under subsection (3), the Corporation shall pay to the Receiver General, within the prescribed time and in the prescribed manner, as an amount due to Her Majesty in right of Canada in respect of mail to which the agreement applies, the greater of the duties collected by the Corporation in respect of the mail and the duties required to be collected in respect of the mail by the Corporation under the agreement, unless
(a) the Corporation establishes to the satisfaction of the Minister that the mail has not been delivered and that the mail
(i) is no longer in Canada, or
(ii) was destroyed;
(b) duties have not been collected by the Corporation in respect of the mail, the mail has not been delivered and a request for a re-determination or further re-determination has been made under subsection 60(1) in respect of the mail; or
(c) in any other case, duties have not been collected by the Corporation in respect of the mail, the mail has not been delivered and the period in which a request for a re-determination or further re-determination may be made under subsection 60(1) in respect of the mail has not expired.
Not public money
(7) An amount required to be paid to the Receiver General under subsection (6) shall be deemed not to be public money for the purposes of the
Financial Administration Act
Interest
(8) Where an amount that the Corporation is required to pay under subsection (6) has not been paid within the time within which it is required to be paid under that subsection, the Corporation shall pay to the Receiver General, in addition to that amount, interest at the specified rate for the period beginning on the first day after that time and ending on the day the amount has been paid in full, calculated on the outstanding balance of the amount.
Detention of mail
(9) Any person who is authorized to collect duties in respect of mail may detain the mail until the duties thereon have been paid to the Corporation.
Fees
(10) Subject to any regulations made under subsection (14), mail is charged with prescribed fees from the time of its importation until such time as the fees are paid or as the fees are otherwise removed.
Payment of fees
(11) The importer or owner of mail that is charged with fees under subsection (10) shall pay the fees at the time of the payment of the duties on the mail.
Collection of fees
(12) Where the Corporation or an agent of the Corporation is authorized to collect duties in respect of mail, the Corporation or the agent may collect the fees with which the mail is charged under subsection (10) and may detain the mail until the fees have been paid.
Fees belong to Corporation
(13) Fees collected under subsection (12) are property of the Corporation and shall be deemed not to be public money for the purposes of the
Financial Administration Act
Regulations
(14) The Governor in Council may make regulations
(a) prescribing times for the purposes of subsection (6);

(b) prescribing the manner of payment for the purposes of subsection (6);
(c) prescribing fees for the purposes of subsection (10);
(d) prescribing mail that is not charged with fees under subsection (10) or prescribing circumstances in which mail is not charged with fees under that subsection; and
(e) prescribing mail to which any of subsections (3) to (13) does not apply or prescribing circumstances in which any of those subsections does not apply to mail.
1992, c. 28, s. 29;
1997, c. 36, s. 190.

Evidence

Proof of service by registered mail
148 (1) Where a notice required by this Act or a regulation is sent by registered mail, an affidavit of an officer sworn before a commissioner or other person authorized to take affidavits setting out
(a) that the officer has charge of the appropriate records,
(b) that he has knowledge of the facts in the particular case,
(c) that such a notice was sent by registered letter on a named day to the person to whom it was addressed (indicating such address), and
(d) that he identifies as exhibits attached to the affidavit the post office certificate of registration of the letter or a true copy of the relevant portion thereof and a true copy of the notice
shall be received, in the absence of evidence to the contrary, as proof of the sending and of the notice.

Proof of personal service
(2) Where a notice required by this Act or a regulation is given by personal service, an affidavit of an officer sworn before a commissioner or other person authorized to take affidavits setting out
(a) that the officer has charge of the appropriate records,
(b) that he has knowledge of the facts in the particular case,
(c) that such a notice was served personally on a named day on the person to whom it was directed, and
(d) that he identifies as an exhibit attached to the affidavit a true copy of the notice
shall be received, in the absence of evidence to the contrary, as proof of the personal service and of the notice.

Members of partnerships
148.1 (1) For the purposes of this Act,
(a) a reference in any notice or other document to the firm name of a partnership is to be read as a reference to all the members of the partnership; and
(b) any notice or other document is deemed to have been provided to each member of a partnership if the notice or other document is mailed to, served on or otherwise sent to the partnership
(i) at its latest known address or place of business, or
(ii) at the latest known address
(A) if it is a limited partnership, of any member of the limited partnership whose liability as a member is not limited, or
(B) in any other case, of any member of the partnership.

Members of unincorporated bodies
(2) For the purposes of this Act,
(a) a reference in any notice or other document to the firm name of an unincorporated body is to be read as a reference to all the members of the body; and
(b) any notice or other document is deemed to have been provided to each member of an unincorporated body if the notice or other document is mailed to, served on or otherwise sent to the body at its latest known address or place of business.
2001, c. 25, s. 79.

Date of notice by mail

149 For the purposes of this Act, the date on which a notice is given pursuant to this Act or the regulations shall, where it is given by mail, be deemed to be the date of mailing of the notice, and the date of mailing shall, in the absence of any evidence to the contrary, be deemed to be the day appearing from such notice to be the date thereof unless called into question by the Minister or by some person acting for him or Her Majesty.

Proof of no appeal

149.1 An affidavit of an officer, sworn before a commissioner or other person authorized to take affidavits, setting out that the officer has charge of the appropriate records and has knowledge of the practice of the Agency or the Canada Revenue Agency, as the case may be, and that an examination of the records shows that a notice of assessment under Part V.1 was mailed or otherwise sent to a person under this Act and that, after careful examination and search of the records, the officer has been unable to find that a notice of objection or of appeal from the assessment was received within the time allowed for the notice, is evidence of the statements contained in the affidavit.

2001, c. 25, s. 80;
2005, c. 38, s. 82;
2009, c. 10, s. 15(F).

Objection or appeal

149.2 If a person who is required under this Act to keep records serves a notice of objection or is a party to an appeal or reference under Part V.1, the person shall retain, until the objection, appeal or reference and any appeal from it is finally disposed of, every record that pertains to the subject-matter of the objection, appeal or reference.

2001, c. 25, s. 80.

Copies of documents

150 Copies of documents made pursuant to this or any other Act of Parliament that prohibits, controls or regulates the importation or exportation of goods or pursuant to any regulation made thereunder that are duly certified by an officer are admissible in evidence in any proceeding taken pursuant to this Act in the same manner as if they were the originals of such documents.

False information in documents

151 In any proceeding taken pursuant to this Act, the production or the proof of the existence of more than one document made or sent by or on behalf of the same person in which the same goods are mentioned as bearing different prices or given different names or descriptions is, in the absence of evidence to the contrary, proof that any such document was intended to be used to evade compliance with this Act or the payment of duties under this Act.

Burden of proof of importation or exportation on Her Majesty

152 (1) In any proceeding under this Act relating to the importation or exportation of goods, the burden of proof of the importation or exportation of the goods lies on Her Majesty.

Proof of importation

(2) For the purpose of subsection (1), proof of the foreign origin of goods is, in the absence of evidence to the contrary, proof of the importation of the goods.

Burden of proof on other party

(3) Subject to subsection (4), in any proceeding under this Act, the burden of proof in any question relating to

(a) the identity or origin of any goods,
(b) the manner, time or place of importation or exportation of any goods,
(c) the payment of duties on any goods, or
(d) the compliance with any of the provisions of this Act or the regulations in respect of any goods

lies on the person, other than Her Majesty, who is a party to the proceeding or the person who is accused of an offence, and not on Her Majesty.

Exception in case of prosecution

(4) In any prosecution under this Act, the burden of proof in any question relating to the matters referred to in paragraphs (3)(a) to (d) lies on the person who is accused of an offence, and not on Her Majesty, only if the Crown has established that the facts or circumstances concerned are within the

knowledge of the accused or are or were within his means to know.

Prohibitions, Offences and Punishment

General

False statements, evasion of duties
153 No person shall
(a) make, or participate in, assent to or acquiesce in the making of, false or deceptive statements in a statement or answer made orally or in writing pursuant to this Act or the regulations;
(a.1) make, or participate in, assent to or acquiesce in the making of, false or deceptive statements in an application for an advance ruling under section 43.1 or a certificate referred to in section 97.1;
(b) to avoid compliance with this Act or the regulations,
(i) destroy, alter, mutilate, secrete or dispose of records or books of account,
(ii) make, or participate in, assent to or acquiesce in the making of, false or deceptive entries in records or books of account, or
(iii) omit, or participate in, assent to or acquiesce in the omission of, a material particular from records or books of account; or
(c) wilfully, in any manner, evade or attempt to evade compliance with any provision of this Act or evade or attempt to evade the payment of duties under this Act.
R.S., 1985, c. 1 (2nd Supp.), s. 153;
1988, c. 65, s. 80;
1993, c. 44, s. 105;
1996, c. 33, s. 39;
1997, c. 14, s. 46.
Hindering an officer
153.1 No person shall, physically or otherwise, do or attempt to do any of the following:
(a) interfere with or molest an officer doing anything that the officer is authorized to do under this Act; or
(b) hinder or prevent an officer from doing anything that the officer is authorized to do under this Act.
2001, c. 17, s. 255.
Misdescription of goods in accounting documents
154 No person shall include in any document used for the purpose of accounting under section 32 a description of goods that does not correspond with the goods so described.
Keeping, acquiring, disposing of goods illegally imported
155 No person shall, without lawful authority or excuse, the proof of which lies on him, have in his possession, purchase, sell, exchange or otherwise acquire or dispose of any imported goods in respect of which the provisions of this or any other Act of Parliament that prohibits, controls or regulates the importation of goods have been contravened.
Possession of blank documents
156 No person shall, without lawful authority or excuse, the proof of which lies on him, send or bring into Canada or have in his possession any form, document or other writing that is wholly or partly blank and is capable of being completed and used in accounting for imported goods pursuant to this Act, where the form, document or other writing bears any certificate, signature or other mark that is intended to show that such form, document or writing is correct or authentic.
Opening and unpacking goods; breaking seals
157 No person shall, without lawful authority or excuse, the proof of which lies on him,
(a) open or unpack, or cause to be opened or unpacked, any package of imported goods that has not been released; or
(b) break or tamper with, or cause to be broken or tampered with, any seals, locks or fastenings that have been placed on goods, conveyances, bonded warehouses or duty free shops pursuant to this Act

or the regulations.
Officers, etc., of corporations
158 Where a corporation commits an offence under this Act, any officer, director or agent of the corporation who directed, authorized, assented to, acquiesced in or participated in the commission of the offence is a party to and guilty of the offence and is liable on conviction to the punishment provided for the offence whether or not the corporation has been prosecuted or convicted.
Smuggling
159 Every person commits an offence who smuggles or attempts to smuggle into Canada, whether clandestinely or not, any goods subject to duties, or any goods the importation of which is prohibited, controlled or regulated by or pursuant to this or any other Act of Parliament.
Offences re marking of goods
159.1 No person shall
(a) fail to mark imported goods in the manner referred to in section 35.01;
(b) mark imported goods in a deceptive manner so as to mislead another person as to the country of origin or geographic origin of the goods; or
(c) with intent to conceal the information given by or contained in the mark, alter, deface, remove or destroy a mark on imported goods made as required by the regulations made under subsection 19(2) of the
Customs Tariff
1993, c. 44, s. 106;
1997, c. 36, s. 191;
2001, c. 25, s. 81.
General offence and punishment
160 (1) Every person who contravenes section 11, 12, 13, 15 or 16, subsection 20(1), section 31 or 40, subsection 43(2), 95(1) or (3), 103(3) or 107(2) or section 153, 155, 156 or 159.1 or commits an offence under section 159 or knowingly contravenes an order referred to in subsection 107(11)
(a) is guilty of an offence punishable on summary conviction and liable to a fine of not more than fifty thousand dollars or to imprisonment for a term not exceeding six months or to both that fine and that imprisonment; or
(b) is guilty of an indictable offence and liable to a fine of not more than five hundred thousand dollars or to imprisonment for a term not exceeding five years or to both that fine and that imprisonment.
Court order — subsection 43(2)
(2) If a person has been convicted by a court of an offence under subsection (1) for a contravention of subsection 43(2), the court may make any order that it considers appropriate in order to enforce compliance with that subsection.
R.S., 1985, c. 1 (2nd Supp.), s. 160;
1993, c. 25, s. 88, c. 44, s. 107;
2001, c. 25, s. 82.
Penalty for hindering an officer
160.1 Every person who contravenes section 153.1 is guilty of an offence and, in addition to any penalty otherwise provided, is liable on summary conviction to
(a) a fine of not less than $1,000 and not more than $25,000; or
(b) both a fine described in paragraph (a) and imprisonment for a term not exceeding twelve months.
2001, c. 17, s. 256.
Summary conviction offence and punishment
161 Every person who contravenes any of the provisions of this Act not otherwise provided for in section 160 is guilty of an offence punishable on summary conviction and liable to a fine of not more than twenty-five thousand dollars and not less than one thousand dollars or to imprisonment for a term not exceeding six months or to both fine and imprisonment.
R.S., 1985, c. 1 (2nd Supp.), s. 161;
2001, c. 25, s. 83.

Procedure

Venue
162 A prosecution for an offence under this Act may be instituted, heard, tried or determined in the place in which the offence was committed or in which the subject-matter of the prosecution arose or in any place in which the accused is apprehended or happens to be.
Limitation period in summary convictions
163 Proceedings may be instituted by way of summary conviction in respect of offences under this Act at any time within but not later than three years after the time when the subject-matter of the proceedings arose.
163.1 to 163.3

PART VI.1

PART VI.1
Enforcement of Criminal Offences Other than Offences Under This Act

Powers of Designated Officers

Designation by President
163.4 (1) The President may designate any officer for the purposes of this Part and shall provide the officer with a certificate of designation.
Admissibility of certificate
(2) A certificate of designation is admissible in evidence as proof of an officer's designation without proof of the signature or official character of the person appearing to have signed it.
1998, c. 7, s. 1;
2005, c. 38, s. 83.
Powers of designated officers
163.5 (1) In addition to the powers conferred on an officer for the enforcement of this Act, a designated officer who is at a customs office and is performing the normal duties of an officer or is acting in accordance with section 99.1 has, in relation to a criminal offence under any other Act of Parliament, the powers and obligations of a peace officer under sections 495 to 497 of the Criminal Code
Impaired driving offences
(2) A designated officer who is at a customs office performing the normal duties of an officer or is acting in accordance with section 99.1 has the powers and obligations of a peace officer under sections 254 and 256 of the
Criminal Code
peace officer
Power to detain
(3) A designated officer who arrests a person in the exercise of the powers conferred under subsection (1) may detain the person until the person can be placed in the custody of a peace officer referred to in paragraph (c) of the definition
peace officer
Criminal Code
Limitation on powers
(4) A designated officer may not use any power conferred on the officer for the enforcement of this Act for the sole purpose of looking for evidence of a criminal offence under any other Act of Parliament.
1998, c. 7, s. 1;
2001, c. 25, s. 84;
2008, c. 6, s. 59.

PART VII

PART VII
Regulations

Regulations
164 (1) The Governor in Council may make regulations
(a) (b) (c) requiring the payment of costs incurred for the inspection of records held in a place outside of Canada and respecting the manner of determining those costs and the time and manner in which the costs must be paid;
(d) authorizing the collection of information or evidence in order to facilitate the determination of whether any duties are owing or may become owing on imported goods and the amount of such duties;
(e) prescribing the conditions under which non-residents may import goods, including the bonds or other security that may be required, defining the term
(f) prescribing the methods to be followed in determining the tariff classification of sugar, molasses and sugar syrup, and specifying the instruments, standards and appliances to be used in such determinations;
(g) prescribing the manner of ascertaining the alcoholic content of wines, spirits or alcoholic liquors for the purpose of determining the tariff classification thereof;
(h) prescribing how the coasting trade shall be regulated in any case or class of cases and exempting any case or class of cases, subject to any condition that the Governor in Council sees fit to impose, from any of the requirements of this Act that the Governor in Council deems it inexpedient to enforce with respect to vessels engaged in such trade;
(h.1) defining any term or expression that is by any provision of this Act to have a meaning assigned by regulation;
(h.2) respecting the sale of alcohol, a tobacco product, raw leaf tobacco, specially denatured alcohol or a restricted formulation detained, seized, abandoned or forfeited under this Act;
(i) prescribing anything that is by any provision of this Act to be prescribed by the Governor in Council; and
(j) generally, to carry out the purposes and provisions of this Act.
Regulations
(1.1) The Governor in Council may, on the recommendation of the Minister, make regulations for the purpose of the uniform interpretation, application and administration of a protocol, chapter or provision — set out in column 2 of Part 5 of the schedule — in an agreement set out in column 1, and any other matters that may be agreed on from time to time by the parties to that agreement.
(1.2) to (1.5) Regulations prescribing rate of interest
(2) The Governor in Council may, on the recommendation of the Minister of Finance, make regulations prescribing a rate of interest or rules for determining a rate of interest for the purposes of any provision of this Act.
(3) and (4) R.S., 1985, c. 1 (2nd Supp.), s. 164;
1988, c. 65, s. 81;
1992, c. 28, s. 30, c. 31, s. 22;
1993, c. 44, s. 108;
1994, c. 47, s. 72;
1995, c. 41, s. 36;
1996, c. 33, s. 40;
1997, c. 14, s. 47;
1998, c. 19, s. 264;
2001, c. 25, s. 85, c. 28, s. 30;
2007, c. 18, s. 141;

2009, c. 6, s. 29, c. 10, s. 16, c. 16, ss. 35, 56;
2010, c. 4, s. 29;
2012, c. 18, s. 30;
2017, c. 6, s. 85.

Incorporation by reference

164.1 A regulation made under this Act may incorporate by reference any material regardless of its source and either as it exists on a particular date or as amended from time to time.
2009, c. 10, s. 17.

Prohibition or regulation of importation

165 Where at any time it appears to the satisfaction of the Governor in Council on a report from the Minister that goods, the exportation of which from any country is the subject of an arrangement or commitment between the Government of Canada and the government of that country, are being imported in a manner that circumvents the arrangement or commitment, the Governor in Council may, by regulation, prohibit or otherwise control the importation of goods to which the arrangement or commitment relates.

Bonds and security

166 (1) The Governor in Council may make regulations
(a) prescribing the amount or authorizing the Minister to determine the amount of any bond, security or deposit required to be given under this Act or the regulations; and
(b) prescribing the nature and the terms and conditions of any such bond, security or deposit.

Forms

(2) All bonds required under this Act shall be in a form satisfactory to the Minister.

Special services

167 (1) The Governor in Council may make regulations prescribing
(a) what services performed by officers at the request of a person in charge of imported goods or goods destined for exportation shall be considered to be special services;
(b) the charges, if any, that are payable for special services by the person requesting them; and
(c) the terms and conditions on which special services shall be performed, including the taking of such bonds or other security as may be prescribed.

Deeming provision

(2) Anything that is required under this Act or the regulations to be done at a customs office, sufferance warehouse, bonded warehouse or duty free shop that is done at another place as a result of a special service shall be deemed, for the purposes of this Act or the regulations, to have been done at a customs office, sufferance warehouse, bonded warehouse or duty free shop, as the case may be.

Retroactive effect

167.1 Where a regulation made under a provision of this Act provides that the regulation is to come into force on a day earlier than the day it is registered under section 6 of the
Statutory Instruments Act
(a) has a relieving effect only;
(b) gives effect, in whole or in part, to a public announcement made on or before that earlier day;
(c) corrects an ambiguous or deficient enactment that was not made in accordance with the objects of this Act or the regulations made by the Governor in Council under this Act; or
(d) is consequential on an amendment to this Act that is applicable before the day the regulation is registered under section 6 of the
Statutory Instruments Act
1992, c. 28, s. 31.

Parliamentary Review

Permanent review by Parliamentary Committee

168 (1) The administration of this Act shall be reviewed on a permanent basis by such committee of the Senate, of the House of Commons or of both Houses of Parliament as may be designated or

established for that purpose.
Review and report after five years
(2) The committee designated or established for the purpose of subsection (1) shall, within five years after the coming into force of this Act, undertake a comprehensive review of the provisions and operation of this Act, and shall, within a reasonable period thereafter, cause to be laid before each House of Parliament a report thereon.

Transitional

Definition of
former Act
169 (1) In this section,
former Act
Customs Act
Pending proceedings under former Act
(2) Any proceedings instituted under the former Act before the commencement of this Act shall be continued and completed as if this Act and any regulations made hereunder had not been enacted.
Amounts owing under former Act
(3) Sections 143 to 147 apply in respect of any amount owing to Her Majesty in right of Canada under the former Act or any regulations made thereunder unless legal proceedings have been instituted under section 102 of the former Act in respect thereof.
Goods detained under former Act
(4) Section 102 applies in respect of goods detained under subsection 22(2) of the former Act if such goods are in the custody of an officer at the time this Act comes into force.

Consequential Amendments

170 to 182 [Amendments]
183 184 to 194 [Amendments]
195 196 to 213 [Amendments]

Coming into Force

Commencement
This Act or any provision thereof shall come into force on a day or days to be fixed by proclamation.
* [Note: Paragraph 99(1)(b), subsections 99(2) to (4) and sections 170 to 172 in force March 3, 1986,
SCHEDULE
PART 1

Customs Tariff

PART 2

PART 3

PART 4

PART 5

R.S., 1985, c. 1 (2nd Supp.), Sch.;
2012, c. 18, s. 31, c. 26, ss. 37, 62;

2014, c. 14, ss. 25 to 29, c. 28, s. 27 to 31;
2017, c. 6, ss. 86 to 89, c. 8, ss. 23 to 26.

RELATED PROVISIONS

— 1990, c. 16, s. 24(1)

Transitional: proceedings
24 (1) Every proceeding commenced before the coming into force of this subsection and in respect of which any provision amended by this Act applies shall be taken up and continued under and in conformity with that amended provision without any further formality.

— 1990, c. 17, s. 45(1)

Transitional: proceedings
45 (1) Every proceeding commenced before the coming into force of this subsection and in respect of which any provision amended by this Act applies shall be taken up and continued under and in conformity with that amended provision without any further formality.

— 1992, c. 28, ss. 2(2), (3)

(2) Sections 3.1 and 3.2 of the said Act, as enacted by subsection (1), shall be deemed to have come into force on May 30, 1992, except that section 3.1 of the said Act, as enacted by subsection (1), is not applicable with respect to interest required to be computed under
(a) subsection 34(3) of the said Act on amounts payable under subsection 34(2) of the said Act as a result of failures to comply with conditions occurring before a day to be fixed by order of the Governor in Council;
(b) subsection 66(1), (2) or (3) or 69(2) of the said Act with respect to goods released under Part II of the said Act before a day to be fixed by order of the Governor in Council;
(c) subsection 80(1) or section 80.1 of the said Act with respect to refunds for which applications are received before a day to be fixed by order of the Governor in Council;
(d) subsection 84(2) of the said Act with respect to diversions or exportations occurring before a day to be fixed by order of the Governor in Council;
(e) subsection 87(1) of the said Act with respect to drawbacks for which applications are received before a day to be fixed by order of the Governor in Council;
(f) subsection 93(1) of the said Act with respect to amounts that become payable under section 88, 89, 91 or 92 of the said Act before a day to be fixed by order of the Governor in Council;
(g) subsection 132(2) of the said Act with respect to money received pursuant to section 117, 118 or 119 of the said Act before a day to be fixed by order of the Governor in Council; or
(h) subsection 133(7) of the said Act with respect to money demanded relating to decisions made under subsection 131(1) of the said Act before a day to be fixed by order of the Governor in Council.

— 1992, c. 28, ss. 2(2), (3)

(3) Section 3.3 of the said Act, as enacted by subsection (1), is applicable with respect to interest payable on or after May 30, 1992 and with respect to penalties payable on or after the day on which this Act is assented to.

— 1992, c. 28, s. 3(2)

(2) Subsection (1) shall come into force on a day to be fixed by order of the Governor in Council

with respect to goods released under Part II of the said Act on or after that day.

— 1992, c. 28, s. 4(2)

(2) Subsection (1) shall come into force on a day to be fixed by order of the Governor in Council with respect to goods released under Part II of the said Act on or after that day.

— 1992, c. 28, s. 5(2)

(2) Subsection (1) shall come into force on a day to be fixed by order of the Governor in Council with respect to goods released under Part II of the said Act on or after that day.

— 1992, c. 28, s. 7(2)

(2) Subsection 33.4(1) of the said Act, as enacted by subsection (1), shall be deemed to have come into force on May 30, 1992, except that it is not applicable with respect to
(a) amounts and additional amounts owing as duties as a result of determinations, appraisals, re-determinations and re-appraisals made under Part III of the said Act with respect to goods released under Part II of the said Act before a day to be fixed by order of the Governor in Council; or
(b) duties that become payable under subsection 34(2) of the said Act as a result of failures to comply with conditions occurring before a day to be fixed by order of the Governor in Council.

— 1992, c. 28, s. 7(4)

(4) Section 33.7 of the said Act, as enacted by subsection (1), shall be deemed to have come into force on May 30, 1992, except that for the period before the day on which this Act is assented to, that section shall be read without reference to paragraph (2)(b) and subparagraph (3)(b)(ii) thereof.

— 1992, c. 28, s. 8(3)

(3) Subsections (1) and (2) are applicable with respect to failures to comply with conditions occurring on or after a day to be fixed by order of the Governor in Council.

— 1992, c. 28, s. 9(2)

(2) Subsection (1) shall come into force on a day to be fixed by order of the Governor in Council with respect to goods released under Part II of the said Act on or after that day.

— 1992, c. 28, s. 10(2)

(2) Subsection (1) shall come into force on a day to be fixed by order of the Governor in Council with respect to goods released under Part II of the said Act on or after that day.

— 1992, c. 28, s. 11(2)

(2) Subsection (1) is applicable with respect to goods released under Part II of the said Act on or after a day to be fixed by order of the Governor in Council.

— 1992, c. 28, s. 12(2)

(2) Subsection (1) is applicable with respect to goods released under Part II of the said Act on or after

a day to be fixed by order of the Governor in Council.

— 1992, c. 28, s. 13(2)

(2) Subsection (1) shall come into force on a day to be fixed by order of the Governor in Council with respect to goods released under Part II of the said Act on or after that day.

— 1992, c. 28, s. 14(3)

(3) Subsections (1) and (2) are applicable with respect to goods released under Part II of the said Act on or after a day to be fixed by order of the Governor in Council.

— 1992, c. 28, s. 15(2)

(2) Subsection (1) shall come into force on a day to be fixed by order of the Governor in Council with respect to goods released under Part II of the said Act on or after that day.

— 1992, c. 28, s. 16(3)

(3) Subsections (1) and (2) are applicable with respect to goods released under Part II of the said Act on or after a day to be fixed by order of the Governor in Council.

— 1992, c. 28, s. 17(2)

(2) Subsection (1) shall come into force on a day to be fixed by order of the Governor in Council with respect to goods released under Part II of the said Act on or after that day.

— 1992, c. 28, s. 18(2)

(2) Subsection (1) is applicable with respect to goods released under Part II of the said Act on or after a day to be fixed by order of the Governor in Council.

— 1992, c. 28, s. 19(2)

(2) Subsection (1) is applicable with respect to goods released under Part II of the said Act on or after a day to be fixed by order of the Governor in Council.

— 1992, c. 28, s. 20(2)

(2) Subsection (1) is applicable with respect to refunds for which applications are received on or after a day to be fixed by order of the Governor in Council.

— 1992, c. 28, s. 21(2)

(2) Subsection (1) is applicable with respect to refunds for which applications are received on or after a day to be fixed by order of the Governor in Council.

— 1992, c. 28, s. 22(4)

(4) Subsections (1) to (3) are applicable with respect to diversions and exportations occurring on or

after a day to be fixed by order of the Governor in Council.

— 1992, c. 28, s. 23(2)

(2) Subsection (1) is applicable with respect to drawbacks for which applications are received on or after a day to be fixed by order of the Governor in Council.

— 1992, c. 28, ss. 24(2), (3)

(2) Subsections 93(1), (2), (4) and (5) of the said Act, as enacted by subsection (1), are applicable with respect to amounts that become payable under section 88, 89, 91 or 92 of the said Act on or after a day to be fixed by order of the Governor in Council.

— 1992, c. 28, ss. 24(2), (3)

(3) Subsection 93(3) of the said Act, as enacted by subsection (1), is applicable with respect to failures to report dispositions, diversions or failures to comply where the dispositions, diversions or failures to comply occur on or after a day to be fixed by order of the Governor in Council.

— 1992, c. 28, s. 26(2)

(2) Subsection (1) is applicable with respect to money received pursuant to section 117, 118 or 119 of the said Act on or after a day to be fixed by order of the Governor in Council.

— 1992, c. 28, s. 27(2)

(2) Subsection (1) is applicable with respect to money demanded relating to decisions made under subsection 131(1) of the said Act on or after a day to be fixed by order of the Governor in Council.

— 1992, c. 28, s. 29(2)

(2) Subsection (1) shall come into force on a day to be fixed by order of the Governor in Council with respect to goods released under Part II of the said Act on or after that day.

— 1992, c. 28, s. 30(5)

(5) Subsections (2) and (3) are applicable with respect to regulations made on or after the day this Act is assented to.

— 1992, c. 28, s. 31(2)

(2) Subsection (1) is applicable with respect to regulations made on or after the day this Act is assented to.

— 1993, c. 25, ss. 90, 91(1)

Interest
90 For the purposes of the provisions of the
Customs Act

— **1993, c. 25, ss. 90, 91(1)**

Regulations may be retroactive
91 (1) Any regulation, or any provision of any regulation, made within eighteen months after this Act is assented to, under paragraph 30(l), (m) or (n) of the
Customs Act

— **1997, c. 26, s. 74(6)**

(6) For the purposes of the provisions of the
Customs Act
Excise Tax Act

— **1997, c. 26, s. 75(3)**

(3) For the purposes of the provisions of the
Customs Act
Excise Tax Act

— **1997, c. 26, s. 76(3)**

(3) For the purposes of the provisions of the
Customs Act
Excise Tax Act

— **1997, c. 26, s. 87(3)**

(3) For the purposes of the provisions of the
Customs Act
Excise Tax Act

— **1998, c. 19, s. 262(2)**

(2) Any power or duty of the Minister of National Revenue delegated to an officer or a class of officers by an order made under section 134 of the Act, or by a regulation made under paragraph 164(1)(a) of the Act, before the day on which this Act is assented to continues to be delegated to that officer or that class of officers until an authorization by the Minister made under subsection 2(4) of the Act, as enacted by subsection (1), changes the delegation of that power or duty.

— **1998, c. 30, s. 10**

Transitional — proceedings
10 Every proceeding commenced before the coming into force of this section and in respect of which any provision amended by sections 12 to 16 applies shall be taken up and continued under and in conformity with that amended provision without any further formality.

— **2000, c. 30, s. 161(2)**

Subsection (1) applies to amounts that are payable after this Act is assented to, regardless of when the amounts became payable.
* [Note: Act assented to October 20, 2000.]

— **2001, c. 16, s. 44**

44 For the purposes of applying the provisions of the
Customs Act
Excise Act
Excise Tax Act

— **2001, c. 25, s. 58(2)**

Sections 97.21 to 97.58 of the Act, as enacted by subsection (1), apply to amounts that are payable after this Act is assented to, regardless of when the amounts became payable.
* [Note: Act assented to October 25, 2001.]

— **2002, c. 22, ss. 305 to 308**

Meaning of
305 In sections 306 to 320,
implementation date

— **2002, c. 22, ss. 305 to 308**

Transitional treatment of duties on packaged spirits
306 The following rules apply to packaged spirits on which a duty, at a rate determined by the application of section 1 of Part I of the schedule to the
Excise Act
Customs Tariff
(a) as of that day, the duty is relieved;
(b) as of that day, the
Excise Act
(c) in the case of imported packaged spirits that have not been released under the
Customs Act
Customs Tariff
(d) in the case of any other packaged spirits, this Act applies in respect of them as though
(i) they were produced and packaged in Canada on that day by the person having possession of them immediately before that day and the person were permitted under this Act to produce and package them, and
(ii) if the spirits are in the possession of a duty free shop or an accredited representative or delivered as ships' stores in accordance with the
Ships' Stores Regulations

— **2002, c. 22, ss. 305 to 308**

Transitional treatment of duties on bulk spirits
307 (1) The following rules apply to bulk spirits on which a duty, at a rate determined by the application of section 1 of Part I of the schedule to the
Excise Act
Customs Tariff
(a) as of that day, the duty is relieved;
(b) as of that day, the
Excise Act

(c) in the case of imported bulk spirits that have not been released under the
Customs Act
Customs Tariff
(d) in the case of any other bulk spirits, this Act applies in respect of them as though they were produced in Canada on that day by the person having possession of them immediately before that day.

Transitional treatment of bulk spirits imported for bottling or blending
(2) The following rules apply to bulk spirits on which a duty, at a rate determined by the application of section 1 of Part I of the schedule to the
Excise Act
Customs Tariff
Distilled Spirits for Bottling in Bond Remission Order
Imported Spirits for Blending Remission Order
(a) as of that day, the duty imposed on the spirits under subsection 135(1) of the
Excise Act
(b) as of that day, the
Excise Act
(c) this Act applies in respect of them as though they were produced in Canada on that day by the person having possession of them immediately before that day.

— 2002, c. 22, ss. 305 to 308

Transitional treatment of excise taxes on wine
308 The following rules apply to wine on which tax was imposed under section 27 of the
Excise Tax Act
(a) as of that day, the tax is relieved;
(b) as of that day, Parts III, VI and VII of the
Excise Tax Act
(c) in the case of imported wine that has not been released under the
Customs Act
Customs Tariff
(d) in the case of bulk wine to which paragraph (c) does not apply, this Act applies in respect of it as though it were produced in Canada on that day
(i) if the wine is located in a ferment-on-premises facility or at the residence of an individual, by the individual who owned the wine immediately before that day, or
(ii) in any other case, by the person having possession of it immediately before that day; and
(e) in the case of wine to which neither paragraph (c) nor (d) apply, this Act applies in respect of it as though
(i) it were produced and packaged in Canada on that day by the person having possession of it immediately before that day and the person were permitted under this Act to produce and package it, and
(ii) in the case of wine in the possession of a duty free shop or an accredited representative or delivered as ships' stores in accordance with the
Ships' Stores Regulations

— 2002, c. 22, s. 317

Transitional treatment of imported tobacco products
317 The following rules apply to an imported tobacco product:
(a) if duty levied under section 21 of the
Customs Tariff
Excise Tax Act

(i) the duty and tax are relieved, and
(ii) this Act and the
Customs Act
(b) if the product was stamped or marked under the
Excise Act
(c) the
Excise Act
Excise Tax Act

— 2003, c. 15, s. 59

59 For the purposes of applying the provisions of the
Customs Act
Excise Tax Act

— 2006, c. 4, s. 42

42 For the purposes of applying the provisions of the
Customs Act

— 2006, c. 4, s. 50

50 For the purposes of applying the provisions of the
Customs Act
Excise Act

— 2007, c. 35, s. 209

209 For the purposes of applying the provisions of the
Customs Act

— 2008, c. 28, s. 49(3)

49 (3) For the purposes of applying the provisions of the
Excise Act, 2001
Customs Act

— 2008, c. 28, s. 69

69 For the purposes of applying the provisions of the
Customs Act
(a) section
(b) section

— 2008, c. 28, s. 70(2)

70 (2) For the purposes of applying the provisions of the
Excise Act, 2001
Customs Act

— **2010, c. 12, s. 54**

Meaning of
54 (1) In this section,
implementation date
Application
(2) Sections
Excise Act, 2001
Customs Act
(a) in accordance with the rules applicable under the
Excise Act, 2001
(b) in accordance with the rules applicable under the
Excise Act, 2001
(c) in the manner described in paragraphs (a) and (b).
Effect — paragraph (2)(a)
(3) If a tobacco product is stamped in the manner described in paragraph (2)(a), the rules applicable under the
Excise Act, 2001
Effect — paragraph (2)(b) or (c)
(4) If a tobacco product is stamped in the manner described in paragraph (2)(b) or (c), the rules applicable under the
Excise Act, 2001

— **2017, c. 20, s. 67**

67 For the purposes of applying the provisions of the
Customs Act
Excise Act

AMENDMENTS NOT IN FORCE

— **2009, c. 10, s. 5**

5 Paragraph 12(3)(b) of the Act is replaced by the following:
(b) in the case of goods, other than goods referred to in paragraph (a) or goods imported as mail, on board a conveyance arriving in Canada, by prescribed persons; and

— **2012, c. 24, s. 92**

92 (1) Paragraph 107(3)(c) of the
Customs Act
(c) for the purposes of any Act or instrument made under it, or any part of such an Act or instrument, that the Governor in Council or Parliament authorizes the Minister, the Agency, the President or an employee of the Agency to enforce, including the
Agriculture and Agri-Food Administrative Monetary Penalties Act
Feeds Act
Fertilizers Act
Health of Animals Act
Plant Protection Act
Safe Food for Canadians Act
Seeds Act

(2) Paragraph 107(4)(c.1) of the Act is replaced by the following:
(c.1) may reasonably be regarded as necessary solely for a purpose relating to the enforcement of the Agriculture and Agri-Food Administrative Monetary Penalties Act
Feeds Act
Fertilizers Act
Health of Animals Act
Plant Protection Act
Safe Food for Canadians Act
Seeds Act

— 2014, c. 20, s. 366(1)

Replacement of "trade-mark" in other Acts

366 (1) Unless the context requires otherwise, "trade-mark", "trade-marks", "Trade-mark", "Trade-marks", "trade mark" and "trade marks" are replaced by "trademark", "trademarks", "Trademark" or "Trademarks", as the case may be, in the English version of any Act of Parliament, other than this Act and the
Trademarks Act

— 2015, c. 27, s. 35

35 Subsection 107(5) of the
Customs Act
(k.1) an official solely for the purpose of administering or enforcing the
Firearms Act

— 2017, c. 11, s. 7

7 If Bill C-21, introduced in the 1st session of the 42nd Parliament and entitled
An Act to amend the Customs Act
Customs Act
Report
95 (1) Subject to subsection (1.1) and regulations made under paragraph (2)(a), all goods that are exported shall be reported at any prescribed time and place and in any prescribed manner.
Exception — entering or leaving temporarily
(1.1) Subject to regulations made under paragraphs (2)(c) and (d), subsection (1) does not apply in respect of goods on board a conveyance
(a) that enters Canadian waters, including the inland waters, or the airspace over Canada directly from outside Canada and then leaves Canada, as long as
(i) in the case of a conveyance other than an aircraft, the conveyance did not anchor, moor or make contact with another conveyance while in Canadian waters, including the inland waters, or
(ii) in the case of an aircraft, the conveyance did not land while in Canada; or
(b) that leaves Canadian waters, including the inland waters, or the airspace over Canada and then re-enters Canada, as long as
(i) in the case of a conveyance other than an aircraft, the conveyance did not anchor, moor or make contact with another conveyance while outside Canada, or
(ii) in the case of an aircraft, the conveyance did not land while outside Canada.
Powers of officer
(1.2) However, an officer may require that goods that are exempted under subsection (1.1) or regulations made under paragraph (2)(a) be reported under subsection (1).
Regulations
(2) The Governor in Council may make regulations

(a) prescribing the classes of goods that are exempted from the requirements of subsection (1) and the circumstances in which any of those classes of goods are not so exempted;
(b) prescribing the classes of persons who are required to report goods under subsection (1) and the circumstances in which they are so required;
(c) prescribing the circumstances in which goods, or classes of goods, on board a conveyance, or a class of conveyances, are required to be reported despite subsection (1.1); and
(d) defining the expression "make contact with another conveyance" for the purposes of subsection (1.1) and prescribing the circumstances in which a conveyance or class of conveyances makes contact with another conveyance.

— 2017, c. 27, s. 63

63 Subsection 107(5) of the
Customs Act
(l.3) a United States federal, state, tribal or local law enforcement agent, solely for the purpose of communicating the circumstances of detention and delivery referred to in subsection
Preclearance Act, 2016

Manufactured by Amazon.ca
Bolton, ON